"Rob Hensser cha
love us, he likes u
his love. These princip
God and yourself. Get ready to be moved by God's radical love!"

Jud Wilhite, senior pastor, Central Christian Church

"Jesus taught by telling stories. When you mix principles with stories, you can remember the principles. Rob is a leader and teacher of youth. He leads and teaches principles by being a great storyteller."

Loren Cunningham, founder, Youth with a Mission

"Rob Hensser's words have a way of throwing God into my life. One minute you're gazing apathetically at your surroundings, and the next God is in your face, revealing your sin and his relentless love for you. Thank you, Rob, for opening my eyes to the Creator."

Jeremy Limpic, Onetruth Clothing, www.onetruth.com

"Rob has written a book about the most foundational issue that all human beings face: What is the nature of God's love for me? Rob wrestles with the wrong answers that lead us to keep our distance from God, and shows us the biblical answers that will lead us to deep intimacy with him. This is a book that can show you the way to bring great richness to your life and relationships."

Jim Stier, international chairman, Youth with a Mission

dIVINE OBSESSION

god's

illogical

insane

incomprehensible

impassioned

love for you

DIVINE OBSESSION

god's

illogical

insane

incomprehensible

impassioned

love for you

Rob Hensser

Published by Standard Publishing, Cincinnati, Ohio. A division of Standex International Corporation. Printed in the United States of America.

Project editor: Laura Derico
Cover and interior design: Brand Navigation
Cover photo: Scott Ryan

ISBN 0-7847-1839-3

12 11 10 09 08 07 06 9 8 7 6 5 4 3 2 1

Library of Congress Cataloging-in-Publication Data
Hensser, Rob, 1967-
Divine obsession : God's illogical, insane, incomprehensible, impassioned love for you / Rob Hensser.
p. cm.
ISBN 0-7847-1839-3 (perfect bound pbk.)
1. Youth--Religious life. 2. God--Love--Biblical teaching. 3. Bible--Biography. I. Title.

BV4531.3.H47 2006
248.8'3--dc22

2005028526

To the "bump"—I'm already obsessed.

acknowledgments

I treasure every YWAM Discipleship Training School I have had the absolute privilege of hanging out with. To any of you who have given me a word of encouragement about my stories or shared how God revealed himself to you and changed everything during our week, this book is the fruit of your kindness. You are my inspiration and my great reward. Your lives are a masterpiece. Thank you for enriching and inspiring mine.

To Dale and the heroes at Standard Publishing, thank you for your guidance, for striving for excellence and for believing in this project from the word go—you obviously see more in me than I see in myself.

As full-time volunteers with YWAM, Tricia and I are dependent on our faithful supporters and partners. Thank you for believing in and partnering with us. This is as much your ministry as ours. We enjoy our reward now; yours is eternal. Special thanks to Paul and our Central family, Billy and Pattie, Ted and Nancy, Peter and Carla, Johnny, Bubba and Dodo, Leebay, Kelly, Bob and Katie, Deann—you have been faithful with much.

Introduction

I don't have all the answers. The truth is, I have more questions than I have answers. I used to be a lot smarter than I am now. Man, if only I could have spoken to you ten or fifteen years ago . . . I had it all figured out then. However, there is one thing I know and believe with all my heart: if we can just reach out and touch God's heart, it will transform us. It's all I really know for sure. But it's enough.

I'm not a spiritual giant. I'm a plain, slightly chipped, cracked jar with a busted handle that has been glued back on. I struggle with insecurity and lack of confidence. You probably think that I am building up to telling you that even though I'm a bit of a wreck, God loves me anyway. I'm not.

He doesn't just love me . . . *he likes me!*

Our heavenly Father is an illogical, insane, incomprehensible freak who will not stop searching for us, even when we don't want to be found. He is a relentless pursuer—a divine madman who hunts us down, throws himself prostrate before us and asks us to come home, to dare to believe in him even though we are full of doubt and overwhelmed by our own brokenness. He willingly acts foolishly; he can't help himself—he is driven by his burning passion for us. He is obsessed. A consumed creator who loves chipped and cracked vessels with unswerving devotion and commitment—not after we have pulled ourselves together, but as we are. He's crazy about us, even with our quirks. In fact, I don't think he even notices most of the stuff we are worried about. The Father's heart is for us. Dare to believe, reach out, touch his heart . . . and be transformed.

1

ILLOGICAL

The relentless pursuit of Mephibosheth

How much do you love yourself? You probably weren't ready for a question like that right off the bat, but think about it. And no, it's not a trick question—it's totally OK to love yourself. Jesus said that we should love our neighbor as we love ourselves; so if we don't love ourselves, then we won't do very well with the guy next door. So, how much do you love *you*?

Let me put it another way. Last night as I was lying in bed waiting to fall asleep, I thought about all kinds of stuff. I thought about what to wear the next day, whether I would be cold or hot, wet or dry. What would I be doing? Would I enjoy it? I thought about some things I needed to do a few days from now, I thought about a trip I have to take later in the year and finally I started to think about stuff months and months away and how it would affect me. Any idea what I thought about first this morning? Me. I needed to use the bathroom, brush my teeth and most important, I needed coffee. After I had been up a while, my big belly began to growl—I needed to feed me. Any idea what I thought about during breakfast? What's for lunch?

I am constantly thinking about me. I invest huge amounts of time thinking about my needs. I really love me. So how much time do you spend thinking about you and your needs? Come on—if I put it in these terms, you have to agree that you really love you, right? OK, now let me ask you another question. Knowing how much you love you . . . *do you really believe that God loves you more?*

Seriously, do you really think God spends as much time thinking about the minutia of your life as you do? Do you really believe that God cares what you have for breakfast?

God's pretty busy running the universe; do you really think he's all that interested in what you do in school today?

Do you really believe that God loves you and cares about the tiny details of your life more than you do? Really?

To be honest, I'm beginning to realize that the phrase "God loves you" has a bit of a hollow ring to it. We've heard it so many times it's lost any real meaning. It is just one of those throwaway catchphrases we bandy around the church and plaster on billboards. Sure, God loves me, but God loves everybody and everything—isn't that his job? Perhaps you grew up in a cozy Sunday school and were taught that God loves the kittens and the puppies, your grandma and granddad, the ax murderer on death row, the little flowers and, oh yes . . . he loves you too. Wow, makes you feel really special, doesn't it? Not so much. So we just keep on struggling to perform or pretending that everything is great, when inwardly we are aching to know—does God even *like* me?

I'm not asking if you believe theologically that God loves you. We all know that. As author Brennan Manning says, do you believe that God *likes* you, is *fond* of you? What if I were to say that when you walk into a room, God gets excited to see you? As you draw closer to him, his heart skips a beat. He is so eager to talk with you that he can hardly wait for you to speak to him. And if you decide to snub him and simply walk past, his face falls in disappointment.

Stop for just a minute and ask yourself how the phrase "God loves you" affects you, compared to the idea that God likes you.

---

why is it so easy to believe that god loves the person next to you, your friends and your family, yet so hard to accept it for yourself?

Why is it so easy to believe God's forgiveness and grace are available to your friends in their time of need, but so hard to accept that God would respond the same way to you in your darkest hour? Many of us struggle with deep feelings that we have disappointed God beyond any hope or that we have somehow disqualified ourselves from his grace. We may accept the fact that he loves us in some sterile, benevolent way but feel as though he couldn't possibly like us or be happy with the way we are.

If you've ever felt this way, you're not alone. If we all were to get brutally honest with one another, we would find that most of us (most of your Christian friends) are desperately struggling to believe that God likes us. The very things that make God who he is also make him really hard to get to know. God is an omnipotent (all-powerful), omniscient (all-knowing), omnipresent (everywhere), sovereign, eternal Spirit. But how do you get to know the omnipotent, omniscient Spirit like you know your best friend whom you can see and touch? Which leaves us wondering, how does he really feel about us? The good news is there's hope. Check out this three-thousand-year-old story—from a thousand years before Jesus was even born.

A morning breeze stirs the desert dust covering the chalky, rocky, arid hills in the heart of the Middle Eastern countryside. There's no rolling green grass, just dust, rocks and a few wiry scrub bushes. Over the brow of the hill, mud huts are scattered throughout a valley. Each hut is small—just a single room, with a simple door, a rough window hole in the adobe mud wall and a thatched roof. Mainly farmers and shepherds inhabit the poor, working-class village. A scraggly stray dog pokes his nose around the scraps that overflow from a dumpster. Some of the huts on the edge of town have graffiti strewn along their back walls where kids have tagged their territory.

Looking more closely we notice the huts are gathered around a sprawling building that dominates the center of the valley. Built of stones cemented together with mud, it's basic like the other houses, but it's much larger than anything else in the valley. Someone of importance, perhaps a local ruler, lives here. We stand in front of two large, solid-looking wooden doors. They are unadorned yet imposing, with armed guards standing on either side. The presence of the battle-hardened men makes us feel feeble and nervous. Pushing on the heavy door, we slip into a dimly lit entrance hall. The walls are rough boulders; the floor, smooth stone slabs. It takes a moment for our eyes to adjust to the dim, shadowy hallway after the brilliant sunshine outside. Flickering oil lamps hang along the hall, casting a soft orange hue. Slowly we walk along the stately corridor, turn to our left and find ourselves in a much narrower back hallway. It's darker, and the floor is just compacted dirt. At the far end, on our right, is a plain wooden door.

The door groans as we cautiously push it open and walk into a small, murky, bare room. At first glance the room appears empty, but then we notice a nursemaid sitting in a straight-backed chair next to the door. Her hands leisurely maneuver knitting needles back and forth. She appears lost in thought, staring off into the shadows.

Following her vacant gaze across the room, we see a small boy, just about five years old, crouched in the corner. He is jabbering as he huddles over a roughly carved horse and a couple of toy soldiers. Lost in his own little world, he plays his cavalry game with fixed concentration. He mutters battle commands as he lines up the soldiers and then smashes his horse into them, knocking them over. For a moment we are caught up in the epic siege.

We notice the little guy is dressed in beautiful robes of linen and silk. The colors are vibrant red, blue, purple and gold.

This child must be from a family of means, perhaps royalty.

He lives in comfort, his every need met, but he is unaware of all this as he clashes his toy horse through more standing soldiers. He is enthralled in his game, oblivious to the world around him.

Suddenly a loud blast from the guards' ram horns blares through the residence. The tranquility is shattered as the piercing blast rips through the halls. Panic erupts and screaming people flood the hallways, pushing and shoving in frantic desperation. In the canteen soldiers send their chairs crashing across the room as they jump up to action. The guards grab their weapons and lunge out the door.

The halls are now echoing with chaos. Panicking people jostle toward the exits. Some are frantically trying to gather important belongings; others are rooted to the spot in fear. An elderly lady is knocked to the ground and trampled in the pandemonium. Above it all the horns roar. Finally a sergeant stands in the main hall and begins to bark his orders to the people.

"Quickly—you! This way . . . you, that way, quickly, quickly, the alarm; we must get to safety—it won't be long!"

Back in the nursery the maid hears the alarm and almost leaps across the room. She snatches up the prince and heads toward the door. Confused and disoriented, the boy drops his toy horse and kicks and screams, reaching for it as it spirals to the ground. But there is no time for lost toys. The maid tightens her grip on the squirming child and heads for the hall. The boy cries as he kicks, diving over the maid's shoulder, arms outstretched toward his horse that lies on the dusty ground.

In the halls people collide, thrusting one another aside in their fight to get out. For a moment the maid stands transfixed, lost in the sea of panic.

“Quickly, woman, this way!” The bellowing of the sergeant snaps her back into action. Fixing her eyes on his, she lunges purposefully through the hall. Fear mixes with adrenaline, and the hair on her head tingles. She starts to feel suffocated by the people and the noise, and moves faster and faster in a frantic attempt to escape. As she turns to go into the main hall, with the boy still kicking and squirming in her arms, her foot catches in the hem of her robe. Awkwardly trying to untangle her foot and regain her balance, she lurches forward for two or three strides until finally she crashes headlong onto the stone floor.

A bloodcurdling snap resounds through the halls.

It’s the sort of sound that instinctively makes you feel sick to your stomach—the sound of young bones breaking. The child, pinned between the woman and the floor, screams a spine-tingling howl that fills the building, causing people to halt, just for a second, to see where the noise has come from. The boy thrashes around in excruciating agony, the maid’s body smothering him. She had bumped her head in the fall and lay there unconscious. Finally the screams penetrate her foggy mind, wrenching her back to reality.

She pushes herself off the uncomfortable mass underneath her and struggles to make sense of the scene. The child’s face is red with agony. Veins bulge from his neck and forehead, and his face is awash with tears. His upper body is rigid with pain, yet it twists and lifts from the ground as he thrashes around. Looking down past his waist, she convulses, quickly turns aside and gets sick on the ground. The child's legs are mangled beneath his body. One foot points the wrong way, and shattered bone tears through his soft skin. Exposed muscles twitch, and blood oozes onto the floor. The other leg is locked behind the first, the bone split in half.

A soldier comes to investigate, and even he, a veteran of the battlefield, feels his stomach churn at the sight. But there is no time—they have to get out. The soldier leans over and scoops the child into his arms. The boy howls hysterically, his body stiff as a board with pain. Then he falls limp and blacks out. The soldier kicks the heavy door open and disappears out into the blinding light of the courtyard.

The young prince was named Mephibosheth. He was the son of Prince Jonathan, grandson of King Saul.

Mephibosheth was being raised to rule a nation.

Like his grandfather, he could have one day assumed his place on the throne of Israel to reign over God's chosen people. But in one day all chance of that was ruthlessly ripped from him. The palace had been sent into panic by the news that King Saul and Prince Jonathan had both died that very day on the battlefield. Never again would Mephibosheth know the firm, loving touch and familiar scent of his father's arms embracing him. Never again would the palace be filled with his squeals of delight as his father and he rolled around on the floor, wrestling like great bears. Never again would he ride around the courtyard on his father's back, shouting orders like a great cavalry officer.

The palace had been warned to flee the enemy by a messenger bringing news of Saul and Jonathan's death at the hands of the Philistine army. The inhabitants abandoned the palace to hide in the hills, and in the subsequent chaos Mephibosheth had been injured. But they weren't running from the Philistines. The enemy the palace was fleeing was altogether different. The news was that in the wake of the deaths of the king and prince, a local rebel had staged a coup. This was a nobody from nowhere. He had no royal lineage, no claim to the throne. He was a troublemaker, an upstart who led a motley band of misfits and nonconformists. It was said that he had stolen the crown and audaciously proclaimed himself king! In the political turmoil, he had flexed his military muscle and seized the throne illegally.

This rebel who had no right or claim to the throne went by the name of David.

It was common practice during such rebellions that the revolutionary would gather his army, storm the palace and kill anyone belonging to the ruler's household, thus eliminating the competition.

For this reason Mephibosheth would spend the next long years of his life hiding in fear of his enemy.

While David enjoyed the luxury of the palace, Mephibosheth grew up living on the edge of nowhere in a small rebel camp, constantly watching and waiting for his enemy King David. David had stolen all that could have been Mephibosheth's. Any hope of a bright, purposeful life was gone. Mephibosheth would live every day in fear and paranoia, always looking over his shoulder. Each day was filled with the pain of feeling worthless, cheated by life and ignored by God. All of his family was dead, he was lost and alone, but even more, he was crippled! His legs never healed. He was destined to be miserable and useless, dragging the burden of his lifeless legs like the memories of his hopeless life.

The other kids at school teased Mephibosheth relentlessly, and he despised them right back. He was different. He couldn't play sports or join in the games at recess. When he was older he hated going outside, preferring the shadows and cover of darkness. But that only made things worse. Little kids told stories of the monster that lived on the edge of town and only came out after dark. Even his tribe, the Benjamites, despised him. To them he was a waste of space, a pitiful reminder of what they had lost. The tribe of Benjamin had had a high calling. They were to be the tribe from whom the kings of Israel would come. But that honor had passed to the tribe of Judah, and Mephibosheth was a constant reminder of their disgrace. He could have been king, the leader of God's chosen nation; now he sat slumped on a street corner, forced to beg because he was considered unfit for other work. He hated the disgrace of being on show in front of people who only judged and condemned him. He preferred to hide instead in the dark, shadowy corners of his fear, guilt, shame and deep feelings of inadequacy.

Mephibosheth grew up in a town called Lo Debar, which means "barren place." Not only did he grow up in a barren place, his heart was a barren place. Surely Mephibosheth hated the David we all know and sing about in church . . . and I'll bet he hated God too. If God would allow this to happen to a helpless five-year-old boy, then Mephibosheth probably didn't want anything to do with him. He lived in constant fear of being hunted down by his enemy. Every morning Mephibosheth would open his morning paper with cynical hope that perhaps today would be the day the headlines would tell of David's death as he led the armies of Israel out to war. Perhaps today he would read that David had fallen.

Mephibosheth prayed for David to die in battle, as he *should* have died in battle all those years ago.

On the fateful day that Saul led Israel to fight the Philistines, David was one of the commanders in Saul's army. But David wasn't at the battle; he had neglected his national duty and was absent without leave. In fact, David was living with the enemy! Jonathan had stepped into David's role and been killed in the line of duty. But it should have been David, not Jonathan. Jonathan should still have been alive; Mephibosheth should still have his father and a royal destiny. If only David would die now as he should have died protecting Saul!

How many nights did Mephibosheth cry himself to sleep, pounding his pillow in frustration? He should have been somebody—not this worthless, miserable, crippled man. He should have had a father with whom he could play ball, someone to watch his sports games, someone to talk to when he felt lost and alone. He longed for a father to love him and be proud of him for who he was.

The knock at the door made him stiffen; the hair on the back of his neck stood up straight and his ears pricked up. He hated that sensation, but it happened whenever someone knocked. He felt the cold chill of fear run through his veins. He had spent his life living like this; suspicion and paranoia were his old friends.

Who could that be? Cautiously he cracked the door, his heart thumping in his chest. The face was familiar, but it seemed drawn and anxious. Mephibosheth felt the knot in his stomach tighten as he anticipated bad news.

"You have been summoned to the palace of King David."

A wave of nausea crashed over Mephibosheth. He stumbled and fell backwards, his mind reeling.

How did he find me? I've been so careful . . . what does he want with me anyway? Isn't my life punishment enough? Why drag me to the palace to disgrace me? Couldn't David at least have the decency to come out here and kill me in obscurity?

But there was no choice. The king commanded; he must go.

In the throne room, before his lifelong enemy for the very first time, Mephibosheth stood awkwardly rocking back and forth on his crutches, his arms quivering from the strain. A guard prodded him in the back, and he staggered down the aisle. He grimaced in pain. His insides were churning and his hands trembled. On the outside he struggled to maintain a determined facade of pride, but inside he felt dirty and worthless. Confusion and frustration overwhelmed him. He felt as if he were five years old again. He longed for his father to storm through the doors behind him, sweep him into his protective, loving embrace and rescue him. But his father was not coming.

Mephibosheth stumbled forward, finally reaching the foot of the throne. Unable to hold himself up any longer under the emotional strain, he lost control of his crutches and plummeted to the floor. As he tried to lift himself off the stone floor, the feelings of frustration, guilt and inadequacy began to boil within him.

suddenly the years of pain broke through in torrents, and he erupted like a volcano.

He writhed and heaved on the ground, wailing at the top of his voice as the floodgates broke open. He hated to appear weak in front of his judge, but he could not restrain himself. Again and again he gasped, trying to catch his breath and push out a few words.

It was the king who spoke instead. "Restore everything to this man and from this day he will eat at my table!"

What? What did David just say? There was a stunned silence. Mephibosheth's jaw hung open; had he lost his hearing as well as the use of his legs? Surely the king hadn't just said what it sounded like he said. Maybe King David was making a joke—mocking his unfortunate rival before he killed him.

But no one else was laughing. As soon as the king had spoken, his servants scurried over, picked Mephibosheth up from the floor and carried him to a seat of honor close to David's throne. The emotion of the moment was all too much for Mephibosheth. Tears streamed down his face. Finally, he blurted out, "What do you want with a dead dog like me?"

The phrase "a dead dog" was the worst form of derision in his culture. A dead, mangy, stray, street dog was worthless—the lowest kind of garbage. In essence Mephibosheth was asking, "What do you want with a worthless piece of garbage like me? Why would you even dirty your throne room bringing me in here? Why would you even bother with an insignificant, unwanted, unlovely castoff?"

He had been so sure that David was the enemy who ruled with an iron fist from a distant throne, waiting for anyone to step out of line. He struggled as the feelings of bitterness, fear and distrust ebbed from him.

He would never have believed that he could find acceptance and favor in the eyes of David—he thought that was only for the special few. How could he have been so wrong?

But this isn't just a story about Mephibosheth. It is a story about me as I continue to act like Mephibosheth. And it's not just a story about me; it's a story about the Father's heart.

OBSESSIVE BEHAVIOR

1. Do you think God is intimately involved in our lives, or does he leave us to take care of some things on our own? What does the Bible say about this?

2. Is it easy to believe God loves you but hard to believe he likes you? Why?

3. How would things be different if you fully believed, without the slightest doubt, that God likes you?

4. What can you do to believe that God likes you?

5. Do you think intimacy with God is only for a special few? What does the Bible say about this?

6. Read 2 Samuel 4:4; 9:1-13. Can you relate to Mephibosheth and his story in any way? How?

7. Are there any areas in your life in which you have been hiding in the shadows, in fear, guilt, shame or feelings of inadequacy? Will you trust God with them?

Jot down a few things you don't want to forget from this chapter.

1.

2.

3.

RELENTLESS PURSUIT

Father, I want my life for you to be as fanatical as yours is for mine, so I commit to . . .

Spend a few minutes talking to God about how you feel. List some specific prayer needs and action points that will help you live out the truths in this chapter.

2

INSEPARABLE

The father consumed with his wayward son

I'll be honest with you, I often find myself hiding in the shadows and dark corners, imprisoned by fear and my feelings of shame and guilt—afraid that I am not good enough for God. I feel insecure, struggling with the thoughts that I have disqualified myself from his acceptance or joy. I think many of us know what it's like to be in Mephibosheth's shoes—living in condemnation, afraid to get too close to the King for fear of what he will say. We are afraid he will focus on the things we focus on—the areas where we feel we are just not good enough, smart enough or pretty enough, the times we have failed. So often I feel like I have stumbled from one failure or disappointment to another. I know my inner inadequacies and hang-ups and struggle to believe that God could be pleased with the way I have turned out. I mean, if *I* feel like I have let him down, how much more must *he* feel that?

What about you? What is your perception of the King? We are so wrapped up in our perceptions that when Jesus does finally break in, we don't even recognize him. It's not that Mephibosheth was misinformed about David. He knew all of his characteristics. He knew David was courageous, loyal, just and fiercely passionate. In the same way, we know about God. We know he is just, loyal, jealous and even forgiving. I know his characteristics, but which of these characteristics will I encounter when I appear before him?

The real issue is, how will God respond to me in my moment of need? Why is it so easy for me to believe God's mercy and forgiveness for others but so hard to believe that the same might be offered to me?

The greatest stumbling block to faith that lies in our path is not the often talked about entanglements that come with success, popularity or power, but instead our deep feelings of self-rejection. Sure, Mephibosheth knew about David, but what he didn't know was how David would relate to him in his brokenness and shame.

The truth is there was never any reason to fear. There was never any need to run and hide. Mephibosheth had been living under a lie, as we so often do. There was another chapter to Mephibosheth's story. Many years before he was born, because of their deep love and commitment to one another, David and Jonathan had entered into a solemn promise called a covenant. A covenant was an unbreakable promise of protection and provision, an intimate relationship that was closer than family. In entering into this covenant, David promised always to protect and provide for Jonathan's family, to seek to shower his family with kindness.

Mephibosheth had this protection all the time, but he never knew it; he was ignorant of his birthright. Every day he lived in shame and fear was a day he could have lived in acceptance and peace. Nothing could change that promise David made, not even Jonathan's death. It was such a strong promise that while Mephibosheth had been hiding in the shadows, David searched for him, intent on showering him with kindness.

This is God's heart for us. We must never let our self-perceptions cloud the incredible mystery that we are welcomed and desired by the Father.

Just like Mephibosheth, we have another chapter to our story. Many, many years ago God came to a man named Abraham, promising always to protect and provide, to shower him with kindness. But old father Abraham struggled with the same problem as we do. It was hard for Abraham to know God. Abraham struggled to trust that God really loved him more than Abraham loved himself. In deep love and commitment God, the unlimited creator and sustainer, promised that he could be trusted, that he would always accept, always forgive and never give up on Abraham.

As with David and Jonathan, God's promise included the spiritual descendants of Abraham—you and me (Galatians 3:29).

Just like Mephibosheth, it doesn't matter how dark the shadows, or how hard you try to hide, you cannot be disqualified from the promise that has been made. You cannot be too broken or too crippled in your spirit. You cannot have gone too far—there is no last chance as long as you live. You can run, you can hide, you can resist and dive into the shadows of your shame and guilt, but it won't stop the Father from searching for you—intent on showering you with kindness.

Many of us think that God is a harsh judge with unreachable standards. That he is an untouchable ruler who sits on his throne, waiting for us to mess up. He's not. He is a lovesick Father who cannot get us out of his mind, whose heart breaks for us, who longs to be with us. We cannot eliminate ourselves from his search. But many of us struggle to believe that God would want to be with us—I often do. We feel broken and disqualified, and so we live in a self-inflicted poverty in the middle of a barren wasteland of despair when we should be in the palace.

---

we live as orphans when we are sons and daughters of the king.

If David, who was just a man, can act in such faithfulness to a promise that no one else even knew about (1 Samuel 18:3; 20:14-

17, 41, 42), how much more can we trust our loving Father to do exceedingly more than we can ask or think?

What did Adam and Eve do the moment they rebelled against God? They ran and hid. They covered themselves up and ducked into the shadows of their fear and shame, hiding from the presence of God. How did the Father respond? He started looking! Not after they had repented. Not after they had proved themselves worthy to be trusted again, performed some great task to earn acceptance, pledged to live in a mud hut in deepest Africa or fulfilled an uninterrupted month of good works. In the midst of their sin and shame, God began the chase, the relentless pursuit to find them and restore the relationship. Perhaps you're familiar with the following chase story from the New Testament.

Zeke was a rancher. His father had been a rancher; his father's father had been a rancher. In fact, ranching had been in the family just about as long as anyone could remember. For generations his family had taken great pride in raising the best beef in the whole Midwest. A cowboy's life was hard work, but it was honest work. Anyway, Zeke wouldn't have traded the beauty of the prairies for the grime of the city, not for a million dollars. Each morning just before sunrise, Zeke saddled up, jumped the gate and bolted out of the yard. He'd ride to the canyon's edge where he stopped to look out at the big sky swirled with deep oranges and purples. He wondered if anyone in the city ever stopped to watch a sunrise.

Yep, Zeke loved the cowboy life. He loved riding in the herd, roping and branding; he even loved sleeping under the stars with the other ranchers as they drove the herd to market each year. Zeke stood on the porch, his cup of steaming coffee balanced on the rail, and looked into the fields beyond. He had come from a long line of cowboys, but his two sons seemed more interested in other things, in a different way of life.

---

zeke sighed. ***were the old ways dying?***

"Sugar, you know it's just a phase," his wife, Sarah Jo, said reassuringly. "We all went through phases when we were younger, but we came out good. Don't fret about them boys—they got deep roots."

"I know, Ma," Zeke replied, rubbing his chin, deep in thought. "I hope you're right. It's just the world is changing, with newfangled ways and modern ideas. Things are changing."

"Come on in and have some breakfast, you big ox. Everything will be fine, mark my words," Sarah Jo said, disappearing into the house. As Zeke followed her inside, he couldn't help thinking she was wrong, but he prayed she wasn't.

Zeke knew the writing was on the wall. He saw it in his youngest son. He tried to include him and get him to love the family business, but the young man seemed to withdraw more and more each day. It had started with little comments mumbled under his breath as he sweated in the hot sun fixing the wire fences, but lately he seemed completely uninterested and disconnected. Zeke's fears were proven right within a few weeks.

His youngest boy stormed into the kitchen one balmy morning. "Pa, I just can't stay here in this flea-bitten, backwards, middle-of-nowhere armpit of a place! Ranching is for country bumpkins; I'm going to the big city to make a name for myself. I want what's mine right now!"

"But, son, what about the ranch? What about this year's herd? I need your help to bring them to market. Besides, I don't have that kind of cash sitting around; I would have to sell the herd early or parcel off some land . . . it could break us." But no matter what Zeke said, the son was insistent.

---

the rejection hit zeke hard.

Instead of galloping to the canyon each morning, he would slowly amble over, lost in thought. He played over in his mind where he could have gone so wrong as to make his son want to leave so badly. Was it something he had done? Was his son embarrassed of him or worse, disappointed in him? The weeks leading up to his son's departure were hard on everyone. Zeke tried until he was blue in the face to talk sense into the boy, but nothing seemed to penetrate. Finally he focused on trying to advise his son how to look after his money and be wise with it. Then again, what did Zeke know about life in the big city? He found it hard to sleep during those weeks.

"How long have you been out here? You'll catch your death sitting here all night," Sarah Jo said sleepily, stumbling out onto the porch. She pulled her dressing gown around her and shivered. Without taking his eyes from the horizon, Zeke stretched his arm around her and pulled her toward his rocking chair. "Zeke, it will be OK. God will take care of us; we'll make it through the year," Sarah Jo soothed.

"Oh, Ma, I don't care about how this affects me. I only care about our boy. He's my heartbeat. How will I live without him? Remember back when he was just knee-high to a grasshopper and he tried for a week to rope that calf? They grow up so fast . . . I would give my life for that boy." Tears were now streaming down Zeke's cheeks. He turned and looked into his wife's round face. "It just hurts so much, Sarah Jo; it just hurts so much."

Finally, the day came. "Where will you go, son? What will you do?" Zeke asked.

"I'm not sure, Dad . . . don't worry about me. I'll be fine," his son replied as he zipped up his bag. He threw his backpack into the taxi, and then he was gone.

The son hit the city with his pockets flush with cash and with the youthful confidence that he knew what was best. But it wasn't long before he was flat broke and his place a pigsty. A real pigsty. He took care of pigs to make some money, but he still couldn't make ends meet.

His so-called friends never returned his calls—not that it mattered, since he had pawned his cell phone weeks ago. He roamed the city streets trying to keep warm. The cold was the worst thing about life on the streets—that and being mugged. He tried the shelters; but they were just as bad, and everyone there preached to him about how messed up his life was, as if he didn't know!

As he wandered, he thought about his dad. He just couldn't get over how his dad had reacted when he left. He didn't preach or judge him; he didn't belittle him or cast him off. His dad had just loved him, even though he had thrown everything in his face and rejected him.

---

a small ember of hope glimmered in the young man's soul. perhaps he could go home.

He thought of all the times he had messed up as a kid and how his dad had always loved him and never made him feel worse than he already did. He thought about how gracious his dad had been during the last weeks before he left home.

He felt horrible; he had been such an idiot. But then he thought, *It's no use. How could anyone forgive what I've done?* He had crossed the point of no return, and now he would have to live with the consequences forever!

Maybe it was hopeless after all, unless . . .

Although he couldn't expect his dad to just take him back, there was a chance he would give him a job. He knew he could never be treated as a son again—he had disqualified himself from that—but perhaps he could be one of the workers. He could work hard and try somehow to show his father he was sorry. It was a long shot, but he was running short on shots of any kind.

It was evening when he started home, but sticking around would just have meant another uncomfortable night in a back alley, surrounded by the now-familiar smells of garbage and vomit. He walked night and day, rehearsing in his mind what he would say to his father. Late in the afternoon on the third day, he was passing through some town—they all looked alike by now—when suddenly a figure came barreling in his direction. At first he felt nervous. *Is this guy coming to me? Who is he pointing to, and why? Wait a minute!*

By the time he recognized the person speeding toward him, his father had already flung his arms wide open. He seemed to fly through the air before slamming into his son, sending the two of them sprawling to the ground. He threw his arms around his boy and kissed him all over. Tears were streaming down his face as he leaped up, lifting his son off the ground with him.

---

everyone in the street stopped and stared in amazement as zeke shouted, "I've found you, I've found you!"

The boy was embarrassed and ashamed of himself. What must he look like? And the smell. He should have at least tried to do something about the smell. But slowly every self-conscious fear was washed away by the torrent of his father's celebration.

Zeke, aware that his son probably felt a little awkward, pulled off his coat and threw it around him, covering his stained and disheveled clothes completely.

"Dad," the son protested feebly, "don't you care about . . ."

"Care about what, son? I've found you—that's all I care about. Come on, let's fire up the grill and throw on some steaks . . . just like old times!"

You probably recognize the plot of the story that Jesus told the crowds in Luke 15. In the middle of Jesus' story there is a famous phrase:

"But while he was still a long way off, his father saw him and was filled with compassion for him; he ran to his son, threw his arms around him and kissed him." Luke 15:20

Reading that verse, I always imagined the father standing out on his porch every morning with a cup of coffee, looking to the horizon and wondering, "Oh, my son, where are you? What are you doing? Why won't you call?" Or perhaps while he was out plowing a field, he would stop and think about his son and how deeply he missed him. Then as he stared at the horizon once again, he saw the familiar silhouette appear in the distance.

Later I realized that this story was not told on its own. Jesus was hanging out with a bunch of people, talking about God's fatherlike heart. The crowd was having a hard time getting what Jesus was trying to say, so he told them in three ways. Jesus knew how much we love the three-part saga, so he released a trilogy about the heart of the Father. (Luckily for his audience, they didn't have to wait a year or more between release dates.)

In episode one Jesus tells a story about a shepherd. As the epic begins, our hero is on a grassy hillside, playing his harmonica while he sits overlooking his flock. The breeze gently blows through his long, flowing hair. Suddenly the camera closes in on his eyebrow, which is raised in grave concern. "Dude, where's my sheep?" Without thinking twice about his own personal safety, he grabs his slingshot and heads off into the wild to search for the cuddly little lamb.

But wait—what is he thinking? He may be a great hero, but he is a useless shepherd.

No shepherd in his right mind would leave a flock of ninety-nine sheep to go search for one little lamb.

Who will protect the flock from the wolves waiting to pounce? Who will keep the flock from taking off in ninety-nine different directions? A good shepherd cuts his losses. Better to sacrifice the one for the good of the many. Our hero may have the looks of Brad Pitt and the muscles (and eyebrow) of "the Rock," but he's as dumb as dirt . . . Joe Dirt. We follow him through his journey until finally he finds the poor little lamb, throws it on his muscular shoulders, heads back to the flock and has a party.

In episode two, *The Lost Coin*, Jesus tells of a woman who has more money than she knows what to do with. She obviously has trust issues, as she won't put it in the bank. The plot revolves around one of her coins going missing. As with episode one, we follow the lead character through her quest as she searches the remote parts of her house, desperate to find this pesky coin. Finding it at last, the woman decides to invite all her neighbors over to celebrate—these people obviously didn't get out much!

One central theme continues through this trilogy: the search. Neither the shepherd nor the woman sat back and waited for what was lost to turn up. Instead, they abandoned whatever they were doing and embarked on the search. The context of the third story then is not that the father sat on his porch looking at the horizon for his son to show up one day. No, instead the father went out into the towns and country urgently seeking what he had lost. He couldn't stay home; he couldn't think of anything else—he was consumed with the search. He couldn't think about feed or fences, his thoughts were obsessed with his son, whatever the personal cost. He searched through clubs, bars and alleyways. Suburb after suburb, town after town. Then one day, in the midst of his search, he saw his son in the distance. He didn't care what anybody thought; he took off running like a madman, threw his arms around his son and kissed him all over. So what is God the Father like when he finds us? He is like a lovesick dad who falls on our neck and kisses us over and over, who just wants to hold and love us.

god sometimes seems really impractical.

He is like that shepherd who abandoned the ninety-nine to find the one or that woman who turned the house upside down and then celebrated in the mess. God is like a man who hires people to work at different times throughout the day and then pays everyone for a full day's work.

God is really kind of wasteful; he dumps his goodness out liberally, spilling it all over the place. His generosity drives us mad! The Father is the limitless creator who holds the universe in his hands yet searches the remote, barren and despised places for us. You are always on his mind. As King David's words to Mephibosheth resounded in the throne room, the Father's words to us resound throughout the universe: "Do not fear. I will shower you with kindness."

Though there may be situations in which people label others illegitimate, there are no illegitimate people in God's eyes. Sure, there are illegitimate actions, but at the moment of conception, God becomes intimately involved with a person and out of his wondrous creativity, he calls forth exactly what he wants. You exist because God wanted one of you, and there was nothing quite like you in the whole universe.

You have a destiny that only you can fulfill; you are special—one of a kind. Your heavenly Father loves you madly and is proud of you.

I don't have kids yet, but I have been to friends' houses and seen their kids' drawings stuck to the fridge. You know what it's like: a little girl draws a picture of a house with a front door and a couple of windows. Then she draws a flower, which is bigger than the house. The sun is purple and the grass, blue. She draws

Mom smaller than the flower, but compared to the house she's big enough to start in the NBA. Have you ever known a parent to look at that picture and say, "Now, that's not anatomically correct. And the sun isn't purple, is it? Just look at this coloring job—you went outside the lines!"

No good parents would do that. No way—they take that picture and slap it on the fridge for everyone to see. Dad takes his latest offering to the office and shows it around to everyone, proudly boasting about his talented child. Of course, everyone else looks at it and thinks, *What on earth is that? This guy's delusional!* But even they know a little child can't do a bad drawing. The kid may get the wrong color and go outside the lines, but her parents love it and proudly show it off.

In your life, you may use the wrong color from time to time or get outside the lines here and there. But when you bring your life to God, he can make it into a beautiful picture, because he loves you. He treasures you and shows you off in Heaven. He is like a proud father calling all the angels over to look.

Well, that sounds great, but let me be transparent with you; I often struggle to believe all this. There are plenty of times when I find it hard to believe that God searches barren places looking for broken me. I can easily believe that he would search heaven and earth looking for *you*, but me—no way. Many times I feel like I am in the kingdom on a technicality. You know, Jesus got carried away and made that sweeping statement that all who are burdened can come to him, and I sneak in under the "all." Maybe now God looks at me and says, "Well, you're in. You found the loophole, but stand over there on the fringes." I often feel I'm on the outside edge struggling to get in.

Any idea what Jesus commanded more than anything else while he was here on earth? It wasn't to repent; it wasn't even to love or forgive. Jesus' most frequent command was "Fear not." Three hundred and sixty-five times (one for every day of the year), in one form or another, Jesus said, "Hey, don't worry, don't be afraid—come to me."

"no one or nothing is more beautiful than I, since God—beauty itself—has fallen in love with me." Angelus Silesius, German-Polish poet and priest

---

When I feel like Mephibosheth—crippled, abandoned and broken, hiding in the shadows of my shame, guilt or fear—the Father searches, shouting, "Come sit at my table. Let me shower you with kindness!"

Sure, we feel unworthy. We feel like we're not properly dressed, not good enough. *God isn't like that,* we think. *It's too good to be true. Anyway you don't know me and what I've done, where I've been. I will never be good enough. I'm lucky just to hang out on the fringes.*

But it isn't too good to be true, because it *is* true: the Father's heart beats for you. He longs to throw his arms around you, kiss you and shower you with kindness.

Remember the parable of the good shepherd? The sheep was not required to find its own way back. It did not have to strive to become unlost—it just had to be found. Sometimes it feels like we are so lost we have no idea how to get home, how to get out of our situation. But we don't have to. All we have to do is be willing to be found. God is the relentless pursuer. He will find us.

God loves an honest, open heart. He loves it when we stop trying to pretend that we know where we are, when the truth is we feel lost and our knees are knocking. Let's get raw with our heavenly Dad about how we feel and let him know, "Here I am—I'm willing to be found." He will run like a madman, not caring what anyone thinks, and launch himself toward you, falling all over you.

He loves you and he likes you!

OBSESSIVE BEHAVIOR

1. What has been your perception of God? Is there anything about it that needs to change? How can you change it?

2. Is the idea of God's relentless pursuit of you hard to believe? Why? What does the Bible say about it?

3. Read the parable of the prodigal son (Luke 15:11-32). Which son are you most like? How can you change the negative perceptions you share with that son?

4. Is there any part of your life that you are afraid to let God see? Do you feel you have disqualified yourself from God's love in any way?

5. Do you feel it is hard to trust God? Why or why not?

6. Spend a moment meditating on the quote from Angelus Silesius. Can you say what he said, about yourself? Why or why not?

7. Is there one main area that comes to mind where you really want to let God find you? Will you tell Him about it?

jot down a few things you don't want to forget from this chapter.

1.

2.

3.

RELENTLESS PURSUIT

father, I want my life for you to be as fanatical as yours is for mine, so I commit to . . .

spend a few minutes talking to God about how you feel. List some specific prayer needs and action points that will help you live out the truths in this chapter.

3

INSANE

The free acceptance of Adam

I'm sure you're familiar with the creation story. That must have been a week to remember for the host of Heaven—imagine the excitement and anticipation as God, who has unlimited creative capacity, dreamed up his masterpiece. He had the ability to create anything he imagined. Heaven must have been pulsing with expectation, every angel swapping rumors, waiting in suspense for the unveiling. After what seemed like an eternity, God emerged from his office, called together the heavenly host and shared his outrageous, exceptional vision. The angels must have listened in stunned awe. God's finest dream, the best the unlimited creator could come up with was . . . a nudist colony!

God's original plan was a community where everyone was naked. Imagine that for a minute. Or maybe not. I don't even like to see myself naked. The thought of being exposed in front of the world is far too embarrassing. Just thinking about it is freaking me out, and I will probably get into trouble with lots of people now for even bringing it up—but it was God's idea, not mine.

While the thought of everyone getting an eyeful of my jelly belly petrifies me, the Bible says that,

---

"The man and his wife were both naked, and they felt no shame."

Genesis 2:25

I don't know if you have ever thought about this (perhaps you're not as weird as I am), but have you ever wondered what Adam looked like? I mean, was he ripped? Did he have a perfect body, gleaming white teeth, a long flowing mane, a hairy chest and six-pack abs? Or did Adam look more like Homer Simpson? Instead of a six-pack stomach, did he have the whole keg? I don't know, but I do know that when Adam stood before God he was completely exposed, yet he felt no sense of shame or embarrassment.

I think Adam's nakedness was more than just the lack of a good-fitting pair of jeans and a T-shirt. He was spiritually bare; he had no deeds or accomplishments to drape himself in. He had no good works or performance to earn his acceptance or justify his position before the holy God. Yet still he felt no shame. God had not required anything of Adam in order for him to be accepted. He was at perfect rest.

Imagine if God had started creation with man. What would that have been like? Man would have been floating around in a cold, black void, alone and afraid, unable to breathe because God hadn't gotten around to air yet. Suddenly a blinding light flashes in his face and burns through his retinas. As he shields his eyes from the searing light, great waves come from nowhere, crashing over him as the oceans are called forth. Panicking and struggling for his life, he is pulled to the murky depths of the ocean. Just as his body gives up the fight, a mighty rumbling shakes the oceans. The sea trembles as an unstoppable force pushes up beneath him. Suddenly man finds himself standing on bare rock as God calls forth the continents. Completely freaked out, he takes off running across the bare rock. *Smack!* He runs face-first into a tree that has just shot up out of the ground. Screaming for his life, he turns to run away when—*Bam!*—up comes another tree as God continues creating the trees and plants. He frantically looks for a direction to run and races straight into a lion that appears out of thin air!

Imagine the stress. Fortunately, it was nothing like that. God spent six days preparing for the arrival of man. That's a long time for God, who could have thrown it all together in a nanosecond. The Father spent time lovingly crafting and perfecting every detail until it was all "very good." It wasn't until his exacting standards were satisfied that he turned his attention to man. Then God even went a step further. Out of his very good creation, the Father selected a small corner of land, which he himself tended, planting a personal garden paradise called Eden.

Finally, the Father did something completely different. Until that point, God had just spoken the word, and everything in creation had come into existence. This time the creator got down onto his hands and knees and began to pull the dust and dirt together, forming man.

---

we have god's fingerprints all over us.

Lovingly and tenderly he personally molded the shape of man with his own hands. Then the Father leaned over and his lips touched Adam's in the most intimate, holy kiss, as God breathed life into him. Adam's chest suddenly inflated as air surged into his lungs for the first time. His back arched off the ground as his body filled with the sweet, humid air. His eyes fluttered and slowly opened. Light streamed into his eyes for the very first time.

The first thing Adam saw as he opened his eyes was God's face, just a few inches from his own. He felt the warmth of God's breath on him. Unable to contain his excitement and pride, the Father was grinning from ear to ear.

The Father slipped his arms around Adam and carefully helped him stand up. He held his wobbly friend until strength flowed into his leg muscles. Adam rose shakily, swaying to and fro as he stood for the first time. Not willing to wait a moment longer, the Father began to tug at Adam, "Come on, let me show you around."

Throwing his arm around his friend, God excitedly and proudly took Adam on a tour of his new home. "This is all for you; here is every green plant for food" (from Genesis 1:29, 30).

In his overflowing generosity, God gave everything to Adam freely and joyfully. He didn't lead Adam through the garden and say, "Now, these are apples. They are sweet; you're going to love these. You can eat them, bake them, make them into juice—but they cost $1.25 each, OK? These over here are called oranges. They are really juicy and refreshing, but they take a little extra to make, so we'll say $1.50 each." It was all a gift—there were no price tags on the fruit.

Nothing was required of Adam; he wasn't obliged to earn or justify his existence—it was pure grace.

Humans were created to live in unashamed dependence upon God for all their needs and wishes. They were designed to simply dwell in the rich abundant provision of the loving creator. Their purpose was to receive and then respond out of the overflowing love and grace of God. As long as people continued to bask in the Father's incredible love and then naturally live out of the overflow, God would fulfill their creative destiny.

Yet that idea goes against everything we hear today. The idea of being dependent is wrong, isn't it? Shouldn't we show some initiative, prove ourselves, assert our independence? We have to take some responsibility to dress ourselves, don't we?

Humans were created to live in perfect rest, assured of God's acceptance and favor before they had done anything. They were accepted just because they existed.

Anything that Adam would accomplish would be a natural response to his assurance that God loved and accepted him even if he never lifted another finger. True rest was living out of his acceptance—not *for* it. As Philip Yancey says in his book *What's So Amazing About Grace?,* grace means "There is nothing we can do to make God love us more. There is nothing we can do to make God love us less." This was true rest—never having to clothe himself, never having to strive to attain the standard for acceptance.

We all have our own self-imposed standards for acceptance, our personal ten commandments, our own ideas of what true Christian behavior looks like. The standards differ slightly from person to person, depending upon that person's spiritual influences. But we each use our lists to rate ourselves. If we are living up to our prerequisites, we feel close to God, accepted and holy. When we don't live up to them, we feel overwhelmed by guilt and condemnation, unworthy of forgiveness or acceptance. We ride a spiritual roller coaster of performance-based Christianity that is exhausting. We long for the rest that Adam enjoyed.

You probably know Adam's story. Everything was about to change radically. Humans were created with a purpose—to receive and respond to love—but we rejected our destiny. From that point, the history of humankind became a story of its search for love. Regardless of where we come from, our skin color, whether we're tall or short, thin or fat, good-looking or plain, regardless of social or economic standing, we all inwardly long for the same things. We desperately want to be accepted. We want to feel special. We want to be loved. Why? We were created that way. We were created to get our needs met by God (Matthew 7:7-11; 11:28). If we reject him, how will we meet this driving need? How can we fill the void?

---

well, that's simple, really; if we don't look to god, we will look to one another for love and acceptance.

This leaves us with a problem. "God is love" (1 John 4:8). If a person rejects God, then he rejects love. So a new kind of love enters the world—love of self—a distorted love that is only really concerned with getting our own needs met.

If you look up the word *love* in any dictionary, it will say something like "an emotion felt for another person, a deep affection." Here are some definitions according to the *Compact Oxford English Dictionary*: "1. an intense feeling of deep affection. 2. a deep romantic or sexual attachment to someone. 3. a great interest and pleasure in something."

If love truly is an emotion or intense feeling of deep affection, then my whole universe spirals into despair. If love is a feeling, then I must do something to trigger that feeling of affection within you. If you are going to love me, which I desperately need, then I must do something to provoke that feeling. I must look attractive, perform according to your standards or fit some requirement to cause that great interest and pleasure.

In this world when we say "I love you," what we are usually saying is "I love what you offer me." We are really saying "I love *me*, and you help the process. You make me feel good. I love what you do for me, how you make me feel." The apostle John said,

---

"Love contains no fear—indeed fully developed love expels every particle of fear, for fear always contains some of the torture of feeling guilty. This means that the man who lives in fear has not yet had his love perfected." 1 John 4:18 (Phillips)

If we have to earn love and acceptance by performance, by whatever it takes to provoke that feeling in another, then there will always be a terrible underlying fear of rejection. What if you don't like me? We are constantly tortured with the worry that we may not perform well enough or look good enough. Mother Teresa spent her life serving the poor in Calcutta, India. She said, "What we all want is to be accepted in our brokenness, affirmed in our weakness and loved in our loneliness; to be relieved of the worst kind of suffering—the feeling of not being accepted or wanted." A woman who saw every kind of suffering said that the worst kind was rejection.

So I lie awake at nights, thinking about what I can do to make you like me, accept me, think I am the best. What should I wear, what should I say? Perhaps I should tell a joke, be a funny guy. Perhaps bribery would work, or maybe I can make myself indispensable to you by meeting your every need. Just tell me what to do and I will do it, if only you will love me.

Instead of celebrating my wonderful individuality, I try to look like everyone else. I have been attempting that suave, James Bond look for years now, but at the end of the day, I am just old, fat and boring! I try to act cool, but how do you define cool? What's cool to one person is very different from what's cool to someone else. So I try to be all things to all people, so everyone will think I am cool. I get so wrapped up trying to meet everyone's different expectations that I don't even know who I am anymore.

What I really want is to be accepted by those who have worth. If the people whose opinions I value accept me, then I can get my sense of worth from them. Have you ever been around someone famous like a movie star, singer or important leader? If you're like me, you acted differently around that person than you do around the kid in your class that no one talks to very much. The star has value. If we can tell people we know a star—wow!—we'll be someone special!

Even if I do find people who say they love me, there is still pain and emptiness, because I don't believe it. It's not me they love—it's my "fig leaf"—the actions I dress myself in. They love the false person I pretend to be to find acceptance.

How can they love me? They have no idea who I really am. I don't even know who I really am anymore. I am lost.

Maybe, just maybe, someone will convince me that he really does like me and accept me, but then I think, *You like me now, but what if I don't do the right thing the next time—then what?* I begin to torture myself, worrying that I may not perform to standard in the future. What if I wear the wrong thing next time, say something stupid, act totally uncool? I rehash every event, picking it apart for potential failures. *They acted differently. Why didn't he smile or say hello? Did I have food between my teeth the whole time?*

Honestly, this is one of my deepest struggles in life. I have a low sense of self-worth, so I struggle to be accepted by everyone. I live the life of a pretender, a phony, afraid to let my true self shine through in case it embarrasses me and leaves me abandoned. Agonizing over how I look, I abandon my cravings to be myself and take my place in the sea of conformity. At times I want to do something crazy and freeing, but am afraid. This attitude affects the way I treat others—either fawning over them or ignoring them as unimportant.

But if I live this life of the pretender with you, how much more do I do it with God? I go about wondering why I lack intimacy with the Father, but I exchanged the life of rest for a life of restlessness. Somebody once said we are no longer "human beings" but rather "human doings," always trying to do the next thing to find acceptance.

But the Father can see straight through our pretending. You've probably heard of the term *Jesus freak.* Maybe you even think of yourself as one. Perhaps you were at youth group and the speaker encouraged you to be one. Perhaps you have the T-shirt that says it, so you can walk around and shove it everyone's face: "I'm a Jesus freak!" That sounds good, doesn't it? Who doesn't want to be a Jesus freak?

We may talk about being a freak for Jesus, but you know, I'm not really a Jesus freak. The truth is, Jesus is a Rob freak, he is a (insert your name here) freak.

Jesus is the freak. He is a freak about us.

He is the one who surrendered himself to mere humans to be beaten and crucified. Think about it—it's crazy. The idea that the all-powerful creator and sustainer of the universe would act like this is far too undignified and unacceptable. The Father is shocking. Dude, he's a freak!

Some time ago there was a man who loved God with all of his heart, soul and strength. His nation used to love and honor God too, but they had stopped doing it. The man prayed desperately for revival in his nation. He attended every prayer meeting and often interceded late into the night, kneeling by his bed, his heart breaking for his nation. He prayed for the Spirit of God to renew, refresh, to move through the land and capture the hearts of the people.

Then late one night, in the middle of an intense time of prayer and repentance for the nation, something strange happened. God spoke. The tears flooded down the man's face as he threw himself onto the ground, convinced that God was promising to answer his prayers. The man lifted his arms heavenward and cried out,

---

"oh, God, please move in this nation. come Lord, come! Lord, I give you my life—I will do anything, go anywhere. God, please use me to help your kingdom come!"

"OK," God replied. "I want you to go down to the inner city. I want you to find the down-and-out, abandoned people; find the homeless, drug addicts, prostitutes, those who have been cast aside like yesterday's newspaper—and I want you to be their friend."

"Is that really you, God?" the man replied, feeling afraid and intimidated. "But God, you don't understand, you've got it all wrong. I can't do that—you're crazy. I don't have the training for that. I wouldn't know what to do or what to say—I'm not a pastor or missionary. Besides, I'm too young, too inexperienced. My gift is for intercession, not evangelism. You know that! I could never do that. I can pray, I can tithe but I could not go to those people. I wouldn't know what to say or do; our lives are too different. I don't even have a testimony . . ."

Night after night the man wrestled with God's call. He tried to ignore it, pray through it and then he even tried to rebuke it. Again and again God called. The man felt overwhelmed. He had grown up in a quiet, safe neighborhood. He had never been to a bar or a club. He had never seen a real, live prostitute. He knew there was a rough area downtown, but he had never been there—not even during the day. This was way out of his comfort zone.

Late one Friday night, he sat at his kitchen table struggling with God. Suddenly he found himself walking over and grabbing his keys. As he locked the front door behind him, he thought,

---

what on earth am I doing?

He walked down the driveway, past his shiny car, his mind reeling with confusion and nervousness. Walking down the hill to the train station, he questioned his every step. What would he do? Where would he go? What was he thinking? Surely this idea was not from God.

Finally a train pulled up. The carriage was almost empty; it was too late for many people to be out. He felt threatened by the night. Two loud, rough-looking youths shouted at each other as they drunkenly fumbled for a cell phone.

The man quietly slipped into the bench seat at the far end of the carriage, slumped down and looked out of the window. His anxious body stiffened. As he peered past his own reflection into the dark night beyond, he saw the familiar silhouettes of his suburb flash past. Soon the outlines were of factories and warehouses. He didn't recognize the high-rise project buildings outside as the train neared its destination in the inner city.

He stepped out onto the platform and pulled his collar around his throat. He felt exposed. Making his way up the escalator, he found himself standing in the bowels of the city. He had never been there before and had no idea where to go. He started walking.

His ears pricked up as a couple of young guys staggering into the road shouted to him. They bumped and fell into one another as they stumbled out of the nightclub on the corner. Turning sharply he walked away, pretending not to hear the slurred cries that chased him down the street. Ducking around a corner, he paused to catch his breath and make sure they weren't following him.

Something tugged at his trouser leg and he almost leaped out of his skin. A drunken homeless guy held his hand upward to beg for a dollar. Our friend's heart was throbbing, his mind racing. Violence, destruction, fear and abuse seemed to assault him from every direction. He yanked his leg free from his captor and ran.

Turning right and then left, he didn't stop until he was sure he was safe. But now he was lost.

---

futility overwhelmed him. *what was the point? This was stupid.*

He was about to panic when he noticed a small alley between the looming buildings. Pulled by curiosity more than anything else, he found himself slowly and cautiously drawn a few steps into the alleyway. As he peered into the darkness, he could just make out the silhouette of a person standing in a doorway. A cloud of cigarette smoke filled the entrance. The man stood transfixed, face-to-face with a provocatively dressed prostitute. Unsure of what to say or do, he stared blankly.

After a few moments of awkward silence, the woman broke the still night air, "Hey, lookin' don't pay the bills!"

Emotionless, she stared right through him; she had seen dozens of guys like this before. They came from their safe, respectable suburbs to live out their depraved, secret dreams, leaving them all behind again when they returned to their clean, pathetic, fake lives. Thrusting his hands into his pockets like a schoolboy, the man fumbled around for words. He wanted to die as he heard himself say, "How much?"

It was dumb, but it was the first thing that came to mind. She snapped back, "How long?"

This was going downhill fast. His head was spinning; everything was so uncomfortable he hadn't realized he was negotiating with a prostitute! Without skipping a beat she continued, "Look, do you have a room, a car—where do you want to go?"

Now he felt like a total idiot. Embarrassed, he looked down and scuffed the ground with his shoe. He dragged his right hand back through is hair. He felt stupid and weak as he searched for words. "Well, actually, I thought maybe we could just go around the corner to a café and get a cup of coffee."

"Whatever, it's your money," she mumbled, giving him a despising look.

They slid into the booth at the café. She lit another cigarette, slurped her coffee and stared out of the window. She didn't want to know his name. She had no interest in idle chitchat. He tried to think of something to say, but it seemed everything just ended in a one-word response. Finally he hit on a common interest. They began to talk, and eventually the conversation flowed. The faint glint of dawn pressing through the grimy skyline shocked the prostitute. She had stayed too long and had to get back. Grabbing the cash she slipped out of the booth and headed for the door. "You're cute," she said. "Kinda weird, but cute."

Panicking, he called after her, "Can I see you again?"

Without looking back she shoved open the door and shouted, "You know where to find me."

OBSESSIVE BEHAVIOR

1. what are your personal ten commandments, your standards for christianity?

2. Do you ever think any of them would make God love you more? why did you come up with these particular standards?

3. Do you do them to find acceptance or because you are accepted?

4. Do you feel accepted by God right now? why or why not?

5. In what areas of your life do you struggle for acceptance? From whom do you seek acceptance?

6. How could daring to believe in the Father's acceptance change those areas?

7. say aloud three times, "Jesus is a (insert your name here) freak." Is that hard to believe? why?

Jot down a few things you don't want to forget from this chapter.

1.

2.

3.

RELENTLESS PURSUIT

Father, I want my life for you to be as fanatical as yours is for mine, so I commit to . . .

Spend a few minutes talking to God about how you feel. List some specific prayer needs and action points that will help you live out the truths in this chapter.

4

INCOMPREHENSIBLE

The steadfast Love of Hosea

The whole next day our friend found it almost impossible to focus on his work. He stared at his computer, but his mind drifted back to the night before, replaying it over and over. It all seemed like just a dream. He couldn't stop thinking about the prostitute—her life, her situation. He tried to intercede and pray for her, but his mind kept shifting back to neutral as he thought about the woman herself. Where did she really live? Did she have family?

When evening finally came, he found himself standing on the platform again, waiting for the train. He went back the following night and the one following that. Weeks turned into months as slowly his life and the prostitute's started to open to one another and a friendship formed. After a few months, they decided to celebrate a special event on the calendar by going out for dinner and a movie, like two normal friends. But this friendship wasn't normal. They came from completely different worlds.

The differences made the situation even more confusing. The more time they spent just talking and being friends, the more the man realized he was developing real feelings for this woman, and not just as movie buddies. Was it possible? Could he be falling in love? He prayed, "God, what is happening to me—am I going crazy? Heavenly Father, what do I do?"

"Marry her," was the reply.

"Devil, I rebuke you! I rebuke you, I bind you, and you have no place here. Now Lord, please speak to me."

"Marry her."

"What? Are you out of your mind? I can't marry her. Our worlds are too different; it's just too hard. I can be her friend, I can pray for her, I can help her with her groceries but this . . . I'm not cut out for this." Tears flowed down his flushed cheeks. He felt overwhelmed by emotion and confusion.

His hands were shaking and his insides churned with nervousness. He looked across the table at his friend as she animatedly recounted a recent event. He thought back to the first night they met, how she had hardly said a word. She had captivated him then and still did now. There was something about her that kept him spellbound, hanging on her every move. Flicking her long, flowing hair from her face, she paused to catch her breath before launching into the next part of her story. If he were going to do this, he had better just blurt it out now or he would chicken out. He tried his best not to allow anything to distract him as he poured out his heart and professed his love for her.

Her eyes widened larger than the plate in front of her, her jaw dropped and she momentarily forgot to exhale the cigarette smoke rolling around her open mouth. She didn't say a word. She just stared at him with a blank expression. Then the corners of her lips curled ever so slightly, before giving way to a full-faced grin. She snorted, trying to contain her laughter, but once it broke loose, she giggled uncontrollably. "Wow, you had me going there; for just a minute I thought you were serious!"

"I was," he replied, feeling a little foolish.

At that, she turned on him like a viper lashing out at its prey. Tears caught at the edge of her anger-filled eyes. Her face reflected the betrayal she felt. Was he making fun of her? Had this all been for his amusement? Did he think he was clever or so much better than she, to do such a hurtful, spiteful thing as make sport of her? She rose to her feet and let loose a tirade of verbal abuse before spinning on her heel. Pushing past a bemused-looking couple, she barged out of the door into the cool night.

He threw a wad of cash on the table and raced for the door in pursuit of her. He shouted down the street after her, causing people to stop and look around. Pretending it was nothing to do with her, she quickened her pace. Frantic and afraid, he began to run, pushing past the curious onlookers. She glanced back and darted across the street. He caught up with her, grabbed her arm and spun her around. Angry tears left black mascara tracks as they flowed down her face. She twisted her elbow from his grasp and began to walk away. Headlights flashed. He dropped to his knee. Her back was turned but she seemed unable to move her feet—they felt like lead weights rooting her to the rain-soaked street.

There in the middle of the road, with everyone staring, he begged her to trust him, to believe him, to marry him.

Imagine how this woman must have felt. She had grown up in the desolate, debauched, devastated wastelands of humanity. She had never known worth or dignity. She felt valueless, unclean and used. In fact, she *had* been used—and abused—treated like an animal without any concern for her feelings. No one had ever asked her about her hopes or dreams. She was a commodity. Imagine her fear, shame and deep wounds of rejection. We see people like this and think, *Why don't they clean themselves up and get a real job?* But have you ever wondered how she got into that situation in the first place? What must her life have been, her childhood, her home—if she had ever had one? Perhaps she was mothered by a prostitute—tossed aside, uncared for and forced to start turning tricks to make ends meet or to support a drug habit. How could she ever trust this man? Would he ever really trust her?

Finally, the day came. Nervously she walked into his safe, suburban home. The first weeks were awkward as she struggled to find her place in his surroundings. He had lifted her out of devastation and despair and had given her a new life—a home of security, acceptance, peace, comfort and love. Her past was well known, but love kept no record. He never mentioned it.

It was early on a Saturday morning. The sun was just peeping in through the bedroom blinds. He rolled over and flung his arm onto his wife's side of the bed. He groped around the bed with his hand but felt nothing. Lifting his head off the pillow, he looked over sleepily. She wasn't there. Scratching his side and yawning, he swung his legs out of the warm bed and into the slippers that sat neatly on the floor. He pulled the belt of his robe tightly around his waist as he stumbled down the stairs. Perhaps she had gotten up early to make breakfast. But the kitchen was undisturbed. He walked into the back garden; perhaps she was hanging out the washing. But the yard was empty. She must have made an early start at the grocery store. But the car was still in the driveway.

He rubbed his head as he shuffled back into the kitchen and sat down at the table. Was he forgetting something? He couldn't remember her mentioning anything. As he sat yawning and rubbing the sleep out of his eyes, he noticed a folded piece of paper wedged between the sugar bowl and the saltshaker in the middle of the table. He opened it and read,

---

"I'm gone. Forget me."

He felt a wave of nausea as if someone had kicked him in the stomach. He struggled to breathe. He didn't know what to think; he didn't know how to think. He felt empty, unable to control the confusion dominating his thoughts. He just sat staring at the wall.

He had done everything for her. He had restored her dignity and purpose, given her a place of safety and peace, a place of respect and value; but she had thrown it in his face and returned to the abuse, pain and violence of the street. What would motivate her to leave a place of comfort for such dark difficulties? Could she not believe it? Did she live in fear that she was the brunt of a cruel joke? Did she feel like a fraud? When she pushed her shopping cart down the cereal aisle at the local grocery store, could she feel the unforgiving stares of other women burning into her back? Was she convinced they all knew who she really was? Did she sit in church on Sunday morning feeling like everyone was whispering about her behind her back? Was she plagued by the guilt of her past? Did the lies keep haunting her, convincing her that she didn't belong in such a place? She could change her surroundings and appearance, but she was still the same worthless prostitute. Was she so afraid of failing this marvelous mercy that she ran?

Her husband—her lover—sat heartbroken and crushed. He felt that life itself had been drained from him. Hour after hour he sat without eating or drinking, unable to feel or think. Bewildered, he looked up at the clock. It was almost 11 PM. He wasn't sure what force compelled him, but he felt himself standing again. He picked up his keys, then slowly walked out the door. He headed once again down the hill toward the train station. He stared out of the window at the now very familiar sights flashing past in the darkness. His mind felt numb, unable to focus or think.

He looked in all of her usual places. She was nowhere to be found. He searched through the back alleyways, dumpsters, shady motels and seedy bars. Holding up a cherished holiday snapshot, he asked a fat, greasy bartender if he had seen her anywhere. The barman laughed at this pathetic, sniveling lowlife. What sort of pervert looks for a woman like her? A fine spray of spit splashed him as the toothless barman laughed in his face.

Night after night he endured the relentless abuse and comments about his "whore" and how pathetic and needy he must be. He plumbed the depths of brokenness and pain. He was a devastated shell. Finally, early one morning he crashed through a locked door into a filthy motel room—rented for only half an hour. He staggered across the room and threw himself to his knees on the floor next to her bedside. With tears flowing, he begged her to trust him, to dare to believe in him and to come home with him. Shame and fear gripped her face as she hid it in the grimy sheets. He threw his arms around her and spoke words of love, acceptance, gentleness and honor over his wife. The guy she had been with laughed snidely as he pulled on his trousers, "What sort of sick, needy weirdo are you? You're pathetic." But these words of derision went unheard, drowned out by the committed words of devotion.

The man's name was Hosea. The story, found in the Bible, in Hosea 1–3, recounts how Hosea searched for his bride, Gomer. But this is not just a story about Hosea and Gomer. It's a story about me, as I continue to fail to believe and run to the dark shadows of my doubt. But it isn't just a story about me, it's also a story about the Father's heart.

Hosea's life reveals a God who yearns for us, who wants us desperately. In the late thirteenth century, the female mystic Mechtild of Magdeburg said,

---

"God burns with passionate desire."

You drive God wild. He is overflowing with love and passion for you. That passion cannot be understood, categorized or boxed into our limiting, preconceived ideas of appropriate behavior. I'm not sure God is all that "appropriate," and I, for one, am glad. The Father is not a sterile, predictable, unfeeling, cosmic ruler—he's a crazy, unpredictable, untamed, passionate freak.

Hosea pursued Gomer because of his deep steadfast love. But his love had very little to do with his feelings at the time. If he had relied on them, he most likely would have said, "Forget you! There is no way I will ever forgive you—not even if you come on bended knee and beg for mercy." If he had reacted to his feelings, he would have hidden in a protective shell of bitterness and anger. There is no way he would have subjected himself to the disgrace of going after his wayward wife.

This sort of extraordinary love and passion confuses me. Yet Hosea serves in just a small way to illustrate the pure, endless love and commitment of the Father to us as we continue to disbelieve and run away (Hosea 14:1-9; 2 Timothy 2:13). Through this account we come to know that the unfailing love of God means a steadfast determination to be true. He loves us with a love that will not let go, a love that will not quit looking and a love that our weakness, sinfulness or stubbornness cannot destroy. We cannot disqualify ourselves from the Father's love for us. It is the greatest power in the entire universe. Nothing can break it.

"For I am convinced that neither death nor life, neither angels nor demons, neither the present nor the future, nor any powers, neither height nor depth, nor anything else in all creation, will be able to separate us from the love of God that is in Christ Jesus our Lord." Romans 8:38, 39

That "anything else in all creation" includes my shame, my guilt, my insecurity, my fears and the dark shadows of my past where I feel I have disqualified myself from God's favor. It includes the stupid things I am going to do today, tomorrow and next year. It includes my weak, stumbling faith, my consuming lack of self-worth and my deep feelings of inadequacy. Even my doubt that he could see anything worth the time of day in me does not separate me from his committed, passionate love. This is the love with which I am eternally loved!

God cries out with love and compassion from the very core of his being. He unconditionally forgives and accepts us because he is filled with an extravagant love for us. I believe there is nothing that gives him greater pleasure than to be with us. The Father was so overflowing with love for us that he came even to suffer at the hands of those he loved so greatly (1 John 3:16).

God's love is nothing like the world's. It is not feelings provoked by our performance; it is a free choice despite our performance. God chose to love us from the beginning of the world, despite our actions (Romans 5:6-8; Ephesians 1:4). God made a choice before time began always to accept us, be patient and kind, not be easily angered, keep no record of wrongs, protect, trust, hope and persevere (1 Corinthians 13). He knows all about us. He knows everything we have done; he knows what we will do. He knows where we will trip and fall; he knows the dark secrets we hide and hope no one ever discovers. Knowing it all, he still made a choice to forgive and accept us—to love us, warts and all. God has chosen to be committed to us in unfailing love, and nothing can ever change that.

There is nothing I can ever do that will make him say, "Oh wow, I didn't see that coming; that changes everything." There is no action or dark secret that will revoke his decision to love us. You can slap God, spit in his face, curse him and die, but it will not change his committed passion for you. He loves you regardless of your actions (1 John 4:10).

There's nothing you can do to make him love you more or less.

Jesus searched for just the right word to explain the Father's heart for us. The form of Greek spoken by the people in Judea in his day had several words for love. One of the ones he used is now familiar to us today—*agape*. You could describe this kind of love as being a discriminating choice. The Father's love is not an emotional response triggered by our performance. It is a choice that he made, with full knowledge of us. It is not based on how he feels towards us. Rather, the choice directs the feelings.

If we base our actions on the feelings of the moment, what happens when the feelings change? My feelings changed about three times before I even got out of bed this morning. How many couples state their reason for divorce as no longer loving each other? What they are really saying is they no longer provoke that *feeling* in each other. They don't fit the requirements to trigger the emotion. The woman looks at the man, remembering how he used to open doors for her and had a six-pack stomach, but now he's a lazy, good-for-nothing slob. The man looks at the woman, who used to spend hours making herself radiant for him, now standing before him with rollers in her hair and no makeup, nagging him about his socks. Each is really saying "I still love me, but you no longer help that process!"

This doesn't mean that feelings are bad or that God has no feelings. He is the creator of emotions and he certainly has deep feelings—but they do not rule him; he rules them.

Years ago I went to Disneyland. The parking lot at Disneyland was so big, there was a train to take us to the front gates. We jumped on the last carriage, and the train snaked through the aisles. Because the train was so long, there were times when the engine passed us, heading down the next aisle as we continued up the previous one. Imagine you are that train. Your will is the engine at the front, and the train cars are your emotions. As you chug along, you choose to change your mind. You have believed one thing, but now you change directions and believe God's Word. (*Repentance* means to change directions.) You head down the next aisle, but there is a period of time before all of your cars make it around the corner. During that time, you still *feel* like you're heading in the old direction. You may think, *Well, I don't feel forgiven.* You have to realize, it takes a while for the feelings to get around the corner and into line. During that time you need to live as if you feel it, because it's true. Regardless of how you feel, choose to believe God, and in time the feelings will get into line with your choice. Feelings must follow choice, not the other way around.

In relationships we don't always feel in love, but we may choose to act lovingly and then our feelings come into line. Depending on the situation, the train may take no time at all to round the corner and line up with your new choice. At other times it may take longer, but you will get there. God's acceptance of us does not change in relation to our performance; it follows his predetermined choice to unconditionally accept and forgive us. The world's love is reactionary. The Father's love is not a reaction; it is a choice made before any action was done. So often I trip in my walk, or the enemy reminds me of my inadequacies and imperfections, and I think, *How will God react to me now?* His love is not a reaction. He's already made his choice, and he's sticking with it. God loves you as you are, not only as you should be. Do you believe this?

It takes a reckless trust to dare to believe that the Father loves us without worry, reservation or regret. The Father's love has no limits. Will you dare to believe, not that he has to love you but that he is crazy about you? That he loves you and he likes you? In his book *The God Who Won't Let Go*, author and retreat director Peter van Breemen says that if the grace of God's love is "offered but not accepted, our life remains under the yoke of inadequacy."

The father's heart is passionately for us as we are.

He accepts me with all my junk. This does not mean God condones sin. He doesn't downplay the gravity of sin. It means he does not abandon me when I fall.

My personal journey toward self-acceptance has been one of stumbling and faltering. However, as I dare to believe that the basis of my personal worth is not my talent, looks, accomplishments or connections, I find myself able to stand before God completely naked and hear him shouting, "This is my beloved in whom I am well pleased!" The more I begin to live like this is true, regardless of how I feel, the more and more the fear of rejection slips out the back door. I am accepted by the Father. I am loved, just as I am. I no longer have to look to those around me to meet my need—I am plugged into the source. God digs me; he likes me for who I am. He longs to just hang out with me—quirky, insecure, unconfident me—and that's awesome!

OBSESSIVE BEHAVIOR

1. How does it make you feel to think that God would throw himself down by your bedside and ask you to come home, even after you'd betrayed him?

2. Do you think God is passionate? What do you think he is most passionate about?

3. Read Romans 8:38, 39. List anything that you have thought would disqualify you from God's love. Ask God if it does.

4. How does the idea that God has chosen you, knowing all you will ever do, make you feel? Does it relieve pressure?

5. How can you live out agape love in your relationships? How would doing this make them different?

6. In what areas of your life do you allow your feelings to lead? How can you begin to tell your feelings to follow your choices in those areas?

7. Imagine yourself standing before God, spiritually naked. Allow yourself to hear him saying "This is my beloved in whom I am well pleased!" How does that make you feel?

jot down a few things you don't want to forget from this chapter.

1.

2.

3.

RELENTLESS PURSUIT

Father, I want my life for you to be as fanatical as yours is for mine, so I commit to . . .

Spend a few minutes talking to God about how you feel. List some specific prayer needs and action points that will help you live out the truths in this chapter.

5

IMMENSE

The revelation of God's name to Moses

My wife's name is Tricia. I haven't met that many Tricias, but a few years ago we worked in a small ministry team that had another Tricia. Let me tell you, one Tricia is a wonderful thing, but two Tricias can be very confusing. Sometimes I would shout for Tricia and get two responses. Often no one responded at all, because each assumed I meant the other Tricia. When people called and asked for Tricia, we would have to go through this process of discerning which Tricia they were after.

We had to find a way to differentiate between the Tricias. We thought about using middle names, but Tricias are very defensive about being called anything other than Tricia. My wife is quite petite so we thought we could call her Little Tricia, but that meant the other Tricia would be Big Tricia, and girls are not too fond of being called "big." Finally we thought about their functions. My wife ran the administration, so Admin Tricia rolled easily off the tongue. But the other girl led a prostitute ministry . . . so the nickname that immediately came to mind there wasn't going to work! It got very confusing.

Popularity of names is cyclical in the West, with certain names fashionable for a season until a new wave arrives. Most names have no real meaning to us; they are simply labels to distinguish one person from another. We choose them based upon what sounds nice or what's popular. But in the ancient East, a name was much more significant.

A name represented the essential character and nature of the person. It said something about who the person was and what he or she was like.

It was very early. The hot rays of morning sun sparkled on the river water. A shimmering ribbon of light outlined the white water lilies. Pollen danced in the sultry atmosphere. In the distance, faint peals of laughter disturbed the still air. The delicate sounds drew closer until the tall rushes leading to the water's edge began to jostle and dance. Three young women waltzed through, making their way down to the secluded riverbank. A girl with flawless skin the color of milky coffee led the trio. Her dark hair swung out as she turned and giggled with the trailing girls. She was draped in a flowing garment of Egyptian cotton, woven so fine that it felt like silk. The gilt edges flashed brilliantly in the hazy morning sunlight. Her companions crouched on the bank as she slowly waded out into the warm river. She hung her waterlogged robe on a thick branch and began to bathe.

"Your Highness, look!"

The attendant shot straight up, focusing on the water and pointing just past a cluster of bulrushes. There, bobbing on the river Nile, was a papyrus basket. One of the girls broke off a sturdy reed and used it to hook the basket as it floated past. The three huddled over their find as they gently lifted the lid. They looked at each other in dazed amazement. A chubby baby lay crying inside.

The princess cooed softly under her breath as she lifted the baby boy and held him in her arms. "Look, it is one of the Hebrew babies. He was thrown into the Nile as Pharaoh has commanded, but the gods have spared his life."

"I will call him Moses, which means 'deliverer,' because I delivered him out of the water."

"But you're not going to keep him, are you?" one of the attendants asked. "I mean, he's a Hebrew!"

Suddenly the bushes rustled. Almost jumping out of their skins, the girls spun round. “Who’s there? Who is it?”

Moses’ sister had been secretly watching over the basket as it floated downstream. She slipped out of the rushes, head bowed, and timidly approached the royal party. “Begging pardon, Your Highness, but shall I get a Hebrew woman to nurse the baby for you?”

The attendants held their breaths, waiting for the princess’s answer. The Pharaoh had commanded that all male Hebrew babies be killed. Would his own daughter disobey? Would she risk her father’s displeasure and anger, all for a Hebrew?

“Yes, take him; I will pay for him to be nursed, and then when he is older, bring him to the palace,” replied Pharaoh’s daughter.

Young Moses grew up with every comfort and privilege the palace afforded. He was one of the lucky few. Outside the palace was another world, a world of suffering and ruthless oppression. The massive sandstone walls of the city inspired wonder and awe with their sheer size as well as the craftsmanship. On the other side of the wall, however, was a squalid slum that spread as far as the eye could see. The darkness of the garbage city seemed to absorb the bright sunlight into its hopelessness. The slum was home to the entire nation of Israel. Four centuries of slavery had taken their toll. Each morning before sunrise, men, women and children trudged through putrid alleyways soaked with sewage, rancid with disease and death, to the soul-crushing quarries and oppressive construction sites. There they would toil beneath the unforgiving sun with little food, water or rest until nightfall, when they would trudge back to their shelters to collapse from exhaustion and pray for deliverance from the nightmare.

However, growing up in the palace was no picnic for Moses. Although Moe lived with Egyptians, he was still a Hebrew and was constantly reminded of his second-class citizenship. Young Moe would often prop his elbows on the sandstone city wall, slump his chin on his clenched fist and gaze down on the slum city. What would life be like if he lived there with his birth family? Anger and indignation raged within him. Something had to be done for these people, but what could he do?

He was just one insignificant kid in a big, intimidating world dominated by fear and punishment.

When he was older, Moses visited the quarries. The enormity of the suffering overwhelmed him. He witnessed thousands of men, women and children toiling in what seemed like Hell itself. Moses covered his mouth with his hand, afraid he would be sick at the sight of human extortion. He couldn't bear to look.

A few feet from him, an Egyptian ferociously beat a young Hebrew girl. He slapped her relentlessly, spitting and shouting abuse in her face. He spun her around by her hair as she collapsed to the ground. The Egyptian looked up and saw Moses staring in disbelief. Crouching down next to the girl, he glanced up, winked at Moses and then launched to his feet, whipping the back of his hand across the young girl's cheek. Blood spurted from her mouth as her neck snapped back. Her body slumped in the dust.

Moses quickly looked all around—no one had seen the act as they scrambled about their work, and no one noticed Moses either. Seething with rage, he lunged toward the gloating man. The years of bottled-up anger, hate and frustration exploded within him. Echoes of racist put-downs screamed in his ears. His eyes bugged out and his nostrils flared. He thrust his fist straight into the man's throat, crushing his larynx. The Egyptian gagged for breath as he crashed to the ground. Moses straddled his victim and beat him.

Exhaustion was the only thing that stopped the torrent of rage and violence. Moses slid to the ground, screaming and crying as the pain flooded out. The Egyptian lay lifeless, his face unrecognizable—swollen and covered in blood. Moses had beaten him to death with his bare hands.

Moses' sweat-soaked robes were splattered with blood. His knees wobbled as he staggered to his feet. He stumbled a few steps. Bent over on his haunches, he pulled at his hair and groaned loudly. He felt the cold, icy grip of fear snatch him as he looked around again to see if anyone had witnessed the struggle.

Panic swept over his young mind, and he began to hyperventilate. He dragged the dead body through the dust and into the ditch by the side of the road. Frantically he shoveled sand with all his might until the body was completely covered. He ran back into the city, up to the palace and into his bedroom. Bolting his door, he collapsed into a corner of the room in terrible fear. He had just murdered an Egyptian in broad daylight. And though he thought no one had witnessed his crime, he would soon find out he was mistaken.

Pharoah would never let him, a murderer, live. He would have to make a run for it.

The years slowly slipped away. The fugitive Moses had fled across the barren wilderness of Sinai to distant Midian on the far side of the Red Sea. The pomp and politics of Pharaoh's court seemed a million miles away from his life now, working as a simple shepherd. It was so peaceful out on the hills, with just the faint whistling of the desert breeze and the muffled munching of his flock. Looking skyward he thought about life in Egypt. The memories were so faded, it felt like a distant dream. Still, he wondered about his family—his Hebrew family.

Many miles away, under the same hot sky, the nation of Israel cried out to God in the midst of incredible pain and suffering. The burden of their bondage was suffocating. People were physically broken and spiritually destitute. In their tremendous vulnerability, their crushed spirits begged God for help. The Father heard their cry and, moved with compassion and love for his children, set fire to a scrawny little bush in the middle of a barren, uninhabited wilderness.

Think about that. What sort of response is that?

The people of Israel are suffering and crying out to God for relief, and the Father's response is a puny bush fire hundreds and hundreds of miles away, in the middle of nowhere. Wow, I bet that made the people feel much better! Very comforting, I'm sure—especially since none of them knew about it. As crazy as it seemed, God had a plan, and a good one at that. The fire was set to get one man's attention—a man who had been living under a false name long enough.

God is a bit of a pyromaniac.

The Father doesn't mind lighting stuff up and watching it burn if it gets our attention. Sometimes he will set fire to our finances and watch them burn to a crisp. Sometimes it is our relationships, our plans, our circumstances, our best intentions—just to slow us down for five minutes so we'll listen to him. At the very moment when we think we have it all planned out, God gets his box of matches. Our comfort, security—it all goes up in flames. We freak out, dancing around, trying to put out the fire and salvage what we can. But it does get our attention.

The flames licked the spindly dry branches of the bush, but there were no plumes of smoke. Moses looked around to find someone to confirm what he was seeing, but there were only sheep. He walked closer to the bush. He squinted. Could he trust his eyes? The flames glowed with brilliance unlike any fire he had seen before, but where was the smoke? *Get a grip, Moe,* he whispered to himself. He rubbed his eyes hard, then opened them wide. Perhaps he had been in this desert too long; he could swear the bush was on fire but not burning up. Standing close to the bush, he felt a chill run up his spine—where was the heat from the fire? He stood in the silence of the wilderness, mesmerized by the dancing flames.

"Moses!"

Moe almost jumped out of his skin. His heart skipped two or three beats. He gasped for breath as he clutched his chest. Who could that be? He spun around, but no one was there.

"Who's that? What do you want? Where are you?"

He felt strangely compelled to look back at the fire. Again a voice spoke, clearly coming directly out of the fire.

"I am the God of your father," the voice said, "the God of Abraham, the God of Isaac, the God of Jacob."

Moses fell to the ground. The color drained from his face and he hunched over his knees, covering his head with his hands in reverent fear. The air itself seemed to tremble as God announced that the time had come for Pharaoh to let his people go. Slowly Moses lifted his head just a fraction and peered at the bush. The grimace on his face changed into a surprised but agreeable stare. Well, this was wonderful news! His people, the Hebrews, would be free of their terrible affliction. The smells and sounds of the work camps filled his senses. The images burnt onto his mind could never be erased. It really was terrific news; on the other hand, what did it have to do with an old shepherd like him? Was everyone getting this sort of treatment? Anticipating his query, God told Moe the punch line. Moe was about to change careers.

Moses stuttered as the words awkwardly tumbled out of his mouth in protest. He had some deep concerns about the whole situation. The first and, quite frankly, stunningly insurmountable problem with the plan was the tiny fact that Moe was a wanted murderer—a fugitive from the law. His face was plastered on the wall at every border crossing in Egypt. He had been featured on the *Egypt's Most Wanted* show several times. If he even tried to return to Egypt, he would be arrested the moment he showed his passport, and then promptly executed.

On top of that, it seemed God had not considered that Moe's influence with the Hebrews would be at an all-time low. Why would they ever listen to him? Sure, he was a Hebrew, but they had grown up in different worlds. He was one of them but *not* one of them. He didn't fit anywhere—he was better off in the desert! Besides, he had tried to talk sense to the Hebrews before. They were so victimized, so hopeless, that they had turned on him. No, it was pointless. They would not listen to him then; why would now be any different?

What about his family? He had a wife and young kids now; he couldn't just abandon them. During shearing season he had missed the kids' first solo bike rides, and he had never heard the end of it. Was Moses supposed to go home and tell his wife, Zipporah, that God had just come to him in a bush and told him to leave his family and go back to Egypt? What guy in his right mind would want to give that story to his wife?

No, it simply wasn't possible. He had responsibilities that he could not walk away from. Someone had to be there to put food on the table, fix the leaky sink and unblock the toilet. He couldn't leave his career and run halfway around the world with no visible means of support. How could he explain that to his friends and family? He seriously doubted that his church would be any support. Egypt wasn't one of their adopted nations. He couldn't go to the missions committee and just say that God had told him to go. It would have to be processed, prayed about and confirmed. They would want to see his strategy, fundraising plans and expected conversions.

Besides, life had just got comfortable. It had taken Moe forty years to get to the point where he felt content and reasonably happy about the future. The renovation on the house was almost finished. He had satellite TV with 242 channels, including 53 kosher ones.

Moses stopped mid-sentence. He paused for a moment. Was he really talking to a bush? The guys in town would never believe this. He sighed deeply, a tear trickling down his tanned, leathery face. The real issue just wouldn't let go, like a splinter in his mind. He remembered back to the last time he thought he was supposed to deliver his people. Things had gone horribly wrong, and he had ended up losing everything and running for his life.

---

oh, God, is that really you? Is this just a delusion of grandeur? Am I going crazy?

Moses felt the struggle within him. Could he dare to believe that God loved him more than he loved himself? Could he dare to believe that the Father would be there to catch him if he jumped? Could he dare to believe in—to hope for—a second, third, fourth chance? He lifted his shaking hands and covered his face as the tears streamed down.

"Here's the deal, God. If I put everything on the line—my reputation, my comfort, my career, my family, my very life—if I risk all of this, daring to believe you, can I trust you? Will you be there when I need you? Will you be there to catch me if I dare to believe? *God, what is your name?*"

Moe wasn't asking what to call God. He knew what to call God. Moses was asking God about his essential character and nature. What was his heart?

"can I trust that you love me more than I love myself?"

He was getting to the real nitty-gritty, as we all have to do at some point: *If I am going to stand up for you when it may cost me my friends, when my boyfriend or girlfriend might dump me, when people might call me a loser; if I am going to follow you when it means making hard choices and sacrifices; to follow that life path even though my family thinks it's foolish and doesn't understand; to leave my security to go halfway around the world to a place where the needs are overwhelming, where there is social injustice, corruption, famine and war—where I'll have to work and work and work, even if nothing ever seems to change; can I trust you to be there for me?*

Even the untamed desert breeze held its breath awaiting the creator's response. Moses shut his eyes. His body trembled. He had never spoken to God with such unrestrained honesty and emotion. Had he angered God? Would he be consumed in a blaze of thunderbolts from Heaven any moment now? Was God even there?

"I AM. I AM WHO I AM."

Huh? What sort of an answer is that? Here's Moe, putting it all on the line, pouring his heart out to God, and this is the response? Is this some kind of riddle? Is it a test of faith? Is God saying that he doesn't have to prove himself; that Moe will just have to have a little more faith without any sense of assurance? Is God an omnipotent, omniscient, omnipresent, immovable, mysterious sovereign who cannot be bothered with the rantings of a mere mortal?

No, what I think the Father was saying to Moses was, "I am it. I am all you need. Do you need acceptance? I am acceptance. Do you need grace? I am grace. Favor, mercy, love, forgiveness, peace, joy, kindness, patience, hope, assurance . . . I AM!"

So, what do you need?

OBSESSIVE BEHAVIOR

1. What names have you been going by? What's your reputation?

2. What have you believed about your essential character and nature up till now?

3. How has that affected your actions?

4. If you are a Christian, what is your character and nature? Has anything about you changed the longer you've known Christ?

5. Look at Ephesians 1:3-14. Make a list of what Paul says it means to be "in Christ" or "adopted." Do you believe it?

6. God set a bush ablaze to get Moses' focus on him. What is God burning right now to get your attention? Are you trying to put out the fire or focusing on the Father?

7. What do you need God to be for you right now? Can you trust him to be that for you? Do you believe he wants to and will? Why or why not?

jot down a few things you don't want to forget from this chapter.

1.

2.

3.

RELENTLESS PURSUIT

Father, I want my life for you to be as fanatical as yours is for mine, so I commit to . . .

Spend a few minutes talking to God about how you feel. List some specific prayer needs and action points that will help you live out the truths in this chapter.

6

INCONCEIVABLE

The revolution of grace for Moses

The foothold looked solid, but it cracked and crumbled under the weight of Moses' foot as he struggled to pull himself onto the granite outcrop. His leg suddenly jerked straight as if he were kick-starting a dirt bike, throwing his weight backwards. He lunged forward and grabbed a few straggly, shallow roots growing in the rocky crags. Finally he swung his body up onto the ledge. Bent over double, he rested his hands on his thighs and gulped the air. Beads of sweat dribbled down his brow. He wiped his forehead with his sleeve and gazed down into the valley far below his ledge on Mount Sinai.

Through wisps of cloud, he could see Israel's campsite in the dwindling light. The ragtag mob sprawled across the valley. Moe shivered, partly because of the cool mountain air and partly because he was thinking about the amazing events of the past few weeks. The mighty superpower, Egypt, had been brought to its knees through the supernatural intervention of God: ten plagues, a sea that stood while the Israelites passed and rocks that became fountains. It was all so incredible, so unbelievable, that Moses wondered if it had been a dream. *Sleep peacefully tonight, Israel,* he thought.

It had been forty days and forty nights since Moe had seen anyone. He had been on a personal camping retreat high up in the mountain crags, receiving divine direction for the nation. Now his eyes rested on the two stone slabs lying beside him. They were inscribed with the commands of God. As he thought about bringing these words to his people, Moses looked again toward the camp in the valley. In the middle of the camp, he could just make out the flickers of what must have been a huge campfire. He squinted and stared more intently. The people looked like ants, but there was a horde that seemed to heave around the glow.

As he stared he felt a growing sense of unease. A nervous knot in his stomach began to tighten. Something was horribly wrong.

---

oh, God, what's happening down there?

Before he even finished the question, Moses had begun his descent. Grasping the heavy stone tablets tightly under his arm, he slid and stumbled down the steep, sandy hillside. His mind was spinning as it ran through the worst scenarios. *How could this be happening?*

His chest was heaving. The cool desert air was like a stabbing knife in the back of his throat. He could not slow down. As he neared the camp he heard the faint, rhythmic chanting of people. The edge of the camp was a sea of animals milling around aimlessly inside temporary pens that had been built from twigs and scraps of wood. The bright glow of the low-hanging desert moon lit his path as he raced between the paddocks. Clusters of tents were gathered around communal campfires, with blankets spread on the ground for people to sit on while they ate and chatted. But the tents had all been deserted. Moses edged between two closely pitched tents and emerged in the middle clearing.

A sea of swarming people danced, gyrated, jumped and stood in front of him. Over the heads of the crowd, flames leaped high into the black night sky. Moses felt the roaring fire's intense heat on his face. Everyone there—men, women and children—chanted in tune with the monotonous beating of animal-skin drums and the shrill blasts of the ram's horn. Moses could feel rage boiling up within him. *What were these idiots doing? Had they lost their minds?*

In the middle of the mob, close to the fire, Moses' brother Aaron climbed onto a wooden platform. The fire lit his face with a deep golden-orange hue. He bellowed to the crowd as he tugged away a linen cloth, revealing a gleaming, solid gold calf on the platform next to him. "Behold your god, your deliverer!"

The people were hushed with awe and fell to their knees before the glowing statue. They stretched their arms out in worship toward the idol. Suddenly, the drums thundered, the horns shouted and the people sprang to their feet, moshing to the pulsing rhythm. Bodies bumped and limbs flailed into one another as the throng of sweaty people heaved up and down as one. Some climbed halfway up the platform scaffold before diving headlong into the upheld hands of the crowd. Spilling onto the throng they surfed the crowd, their bodies passed around from side to side. Everyone was out of control, screaming and shouting.

Moses couldn't control his anger any longer. He flung away the stone tablets he had received from God. Both hit the ground and shattered into pieces.

People ducked and held their hands up to protect their heads, cautiously looking around to see what had made the tremendous crash. Silence spread across the crowd. Dumbfounded, they stared at Moses, who grabbed his robe at the neck with both hands and ripped it straight down the middle. The crowd immediately began to dissipate as people ran for the exits. Moses thundered toward Aaron, who had come down from the platform and was staring at the ground, shuffling awkwardly, kicking the dust with his feet.

Moses grabbed his brother and shouted in his face. He broke into tears and began to collapse. He crumpled to the trampled ground, sobbing. Aaron threw himself to the ground too, stretched his arm around his brother's shoulders and stammered his explanation, "Bro, don't be angry. You know what these people are like—there was no stopping them. They threw some jewelry into the fire, and the next thing I knew, this calf came out!" Moses turned and cocked his head to look up at his brother, at which point Aaron realized how lame he must have sounded . . .

Moses ground the solid gold idol into dust, threw it into the water barrel and made every member of the camp drink up. The whole thing was a national disaster. The people repented, but Moses still felt horrible. The event had opened the floodgates of doubt, fear and disillusionment. The next morning when Moe woke, he felt overwhelmed by hopelessness.

Was leading these people really what God had wanted him to do, or was it just his own imagination? How could he even think God had called him after all that had happened?

No matter what his head told his heart, it just didn't seem to make any difference. He felt lower than a snake's belly. Could he really lead this people? Did he have the gifts, the skills? Why would anyone follow him? He felt so empty, so weak and incompetent. He sulked around the campsite before heading over to the tabernacle.

He slumped in front of the altar and began to pour his heart out to the Father. "What will we do now? If you won't go with us, what's the point?"

Moses assumed that God would abandon his people after this fiasco. They had blown it. God had given them the opportunity of a lifetime by delivering them from their oppressors, and already they had fallen and let him down. How could God forgive and overlook this? Surely he would never be close to them again, never be interested in them again. God likes those who obey him, those who give everything for him, those who live for him with all their hearts, those who are talented and committed—but the Israelites were now disqualified from mercy. They had fallen from grace. Moses agonized in prayer. Was there any hope now? Then an answer came.

"I am still committed to you. I will still be close to you. I still love you."

As he heard the words, there was a fleeting glimmer of hope in Moses' heart. It quickly faded. *No, that's not possible,* he said to himself. *That's just me wishing, not God speaking.*

Again the Father cried out to Moses, "Come, I want to show you something."

"What, Lord?" Moses asked curiously.

"My name."

The questions spun around in Moe's head as he hiked back up the mountain. What would await him when he got up there? Was this really God speaking to him or was his mind playing tricks on him? He made camp and settled in to wait. Suddenly, he felt a rushing wind.

"Then the Lord came down in the cloud and stood there with him and proclaimed his name. . . . 'The Lord, the Lord, the compassionate and gracious God, slow to anger, abounding in love and faithfulness, maintaining love to thousands, and forgiving wickedness, rebellion and sin.'" Exodus 34:5-7

In the midst of his hopelessness, Moses experienced the essential character and nature of God—a loving Father who is compassionate, gracious, merciful, abounding in love and forgiveness. Moses, like most of us, assumed his people had blown their chance for intimacy with God. The Father moved heaven and earth to assure Moses that he is the relentless pursuer who longs to be with his children, even though they sometimes slip and fall. Our Father is a revolution of grace.

A desperate tramp, a convict, had searched for food and finally found someone who would help him. The kind old man even invited him to stay in his house. At dinner that night the tramp noticed the solid silver cutlery and serving plates—enough silver to buy him a whole new life. The housekeeper watched him carefully. "What crime did you commit?" she asked.

The convict leaned forward menacingly, "Maybe I killed someone. How do you know I'm not going to murder you?"

"How do you know I'm not going to murder you?" rejoined the old man. Then he stared intently at the tramp, who suddenly felt a wave of authority and quiet command emanating from his host. "I suppose we will have to trust one another," the old man continued.

"Okay, thank you . . . whoever you are," replied the convict a little sheepishly. "A meal and a real bed to sleep in, ha, and tomorrow I will be a new man."

But the convict slept only a few short hours. When he awoke the house was dark and still. He grabbed his threadbare coat and his scruffy knapsack and went back to the dining room. He opened the cupboard and began to fill his bag with the silver.

The tramp's ears pricked up, and the hairs on the back of his neck stood rigid. Someone was coming. He grabbed his bag and hid in the darkness beside the cupboard. He tried not to make a sound as he saw the old man enter the room and walk over to the empty cutlery case. Suddenly, the man turned and looked at the convict. He was trapped like a dog, his face full of fear and surprise. *Whack!* The tramp threw a jab that knocked the old man clean out. His body fell to the ground. The tramp disappeared into the night.

The next morning the housekeeper sat crying over the empty box of stolen silver. "So we'll use wooden spoons. I don't want to hear any more about it," snapped the old man.

As if on cue, three policemen arrived at the gate with the tramp clamped in irons. The sergeant pranced forward like a peacock, he was so proud of himself. "I had my eye on this man, and when we searched his knapsack we found all this silver." Then with a smug look and a chuckle, he continued, "He claimed you *gave* it to him!"

"Yes," replied the old man, as he looked straight into the guilt-ridden face of the convict. "Thank you so much for bringing him back. But why," he asked the prisoner, "didn't you take the silver candlesticks? Did you forget them? They are worth at least two thousand. Madame, fetch the candlesticks."

"You mean he was telling us the truth?" fumbled the sergeant. "Guards, you heard the bishop—release him immediately."

The tramp began to tremble in disbelief as the old man shoved the candlesticks into his bag. Was this some kind of trick? "Why are you doing this?" he whispered.

"My brother, you have promised to become a new man. With this silver I have bought your soul. I ransom you from fear and hatred, and now I give you back to God. And don't forget—don't ever forget—you have promised to become a new man."

As the bishop spoke, the revolution of grace transformed Jean Valjean the convict into Jean Valjean the grace-filled one. This scene from *Les Miserables* provides us with an awesome picture of pure grace. It is an illustration of the Father's heart—a heart that does not give us what we deserve or just wink an eye and let us off, but a heart that goes above and beyond, giving us even what we don't deserve.

Some say grace is simply not getting the punishment we do deserve, but that's not the heart of the Father. Love compels him to go much further than that.

He rejoices to give us even what we don't deserve.

Not because we somehow made up for our failures, not because he's expecting something in return, but just because his heart loves like that.

The Father does not delight in stuff; he delights in us (Psalm 149:4; Isaiah 65:19). The Father delights to show mercy (Micah 7:19). He is unlike anything or anyone else. He delights to diffuse this merciful goodness, this conspiracy of grace. He causes the rain to fall on the just and the unjust. He is wastefully gracious to us all—just because it delights him, just because it is who he is.

Every other religion, belief or philosophy in the world demands that people pull themselves up to find acceptance from or equality with God. They demand that we keep the rules, work hard, fulfill impossible requirements or achieve some level of enlightenment in order to reach up to God. Christianity is the only belief in which man is not required to lift himself up to God. Rather, a loving Father, whose heart pounds to be with the kids he desperately wants, comes down to us—in the midst of our broken, chipped lives, in the midst of our scrapes and bruises—and lifts us up. It is a revolution of grace—one that will melt hearts, heal wounds, lift burdens, free captives and inspire hope. A great fourteenth-century English mystic, Julian of Norwich, said, "Some of us believe that God is almighty and can do everything and that he is all-wise and may do everything, but that he is all-love and will do everything, there we draw back. As I see it, this ignorance is the greatest of all hindrances to God's lovers."

The revolution begins when we dare to believe and accept this amazing grace, when we dare to believe that the Father not only loves us but also likes us. It begins when we dare to believe that we have not disqualified ourselves, that we are not unworthy, or too fat, too ugly or too stupid; when we dare to believe that there is no need to stand off in the corner or on the fringe. It takes a reckless faith to accept that God is relentlessly gracious and merciful to us—not in spite of our faults, but with them! I often struggle with feelings of inadequacy and lack of confidence. It has taken me a long time to dare to believe that God's grace may be true for me. Please. Don't be like me. Be a part of the revolution today—start now.

---

dare to believe what the author G.K. chesterton called the "furious love of God."

The Father waits with excitement for you to dare to believe, to live as his forgiven, accepted, loved, valued, desired children. You are the beloved, it's your identity—the true you. It is the Father's name for you, and it is how he sees you. Your trust gives him more joy and delight than any other thing. If you want to bless him, dare to believe. It causes his pulse to race and his heart to skip a beat. Trusting the Father's heart means more to him than every sunset or sunrise, every flower, every star—he gladly gives them all just for the chance to spend a few precious moments hanging out with you. It takes a reckless faith to dare to believe. Is it risky? Sure. It's like a little boy who stands at the edge of the pool. He wants to jump to his dad who is in the water promising to catch him, but he's just not sure. The heavenly Father will catch you; you won't fall—trust him. Take that seemingly risky step of faith and jump out as life abundant courses through your veins.

The revolution of grace leads to freedom. We talk a lot about freedom in Christianity, but what do we really mean? I think it means that we are free to fail. Jesus told us his kingdom is full of little kids. We are free to run around like crazy, knowing that if we fall over, it's OK—we can get back up and keep running. Mom doesn't get mad at her toddler who falls over when learning to walk. The toddler doesn't think, *Well, I've blown it. I will never walk properly now; I have let Mom down and disqualified myself from her love.* Part of life as a little kid is falling. But so is getting up again, not worrying about it and running on. In fact, when the fall is really bad, the first person the little kid wants is his mom, to care for him and assure him it's OK and that he should keep running.

God is not intimidated or upset when we fall over and scrape our spiritual knees, but I think he is sad when we are afraid to come to him in those times. I think it breaks his fatherly heart when we trip and bruise ourselves and are afraid to run into his arms for fear of what he will say. Usually during those times, we avoid God, afraid of his anger or displeasure, when all he wants is to hold us. We don't have to be afraid; our falling does not stop him from loving us.

The Father knows we are going to fall, but he also knows that we are going to learn to run and accomplish great and mighty things.

As Moses experienced the name of the Father, he experienced the Father's heart. He would never be abandoned or left alone; the Father would always be with him. Moses could come to him when he fell and scraped his knees, confident of acceptance and grace.

But this isn't just a story about Moses; it is a story about me as I continue to feel that I may have disqualified myself. And it isn't just a story about me; it's a story about the Father's heart.

Theologian Donald Bloesch said, "The prison has been stormed and the gates opened, but unless we leave our prison cells and go forward into the light of freedom we are still condemned in actuality."

He is saying that the prison door has been opened, but if we don't walk through it, we remain prisoners. What is your prison cell? What keeps you from pushing through that door and running and skipping like a crazy little kid in the sunny, green meadows of glorious freedom? Outside that door are clear blue skies and a lush green meadow where you don't have to worry about tripping, but are free to feel the breeze on your face and just have fun. I think I am afraid that if I go out with all the other kids, someone is going to notice me and say, "Hey, what are you doing out here? Oh, I am terribly sorry—you can't be out here." I am afraid that when I run or get crazy, it will look dumb and everyone will notice. What about you? What holds you back?

Picture that cold, dark, little prison cell. You are standing in the middle of it looking longingly outside. You can hear the faint shouts and laughter of other kids. As you stand there, the Father fills the doorway. He is huge and has to duck his head to enter. He walks up to you with arms open, and you throw yourself into them and wrap your arms around his waist.

As the Father holds you, he begins to turn around. You turn right around with him, your face buried in his robes in fear and shame. Then he whispers, “Hey, look.” Slowly, you pull your tear-stained face from his side and look around through blurry eyes. You are no longer standing in the prison cell. You are outside. The sun is shining down on your face, and you can smell the daisies that are scattered across the meadow. The Father smiles and says, “Come on, let’s get crazy!” Then he skips off, waving his arms around in the air. You squeeze out a nervous smile as you take a deep breath. You launch after him, tackle him and begin to roll around in a patch of daisies . . . and laugh.

OBSESSIVE BEHAVIOR

1. what does grace mean to you?

2. Is it hard to accept that God would give us the candlesticks when we have just been caught stealing his spoons? How is that different from what you have thought about God in the past?

3. How does it make you feel to know there is nothing you can do to make God love you more? How do you respond to that?

4. Do your actions show that you believe God is all love and that he will do everything? why or why not?

5. can you dare to believe that the Father will show grace toward you? How do you think this would change how you live?

6. what do you normally do when you make a mistake—run to God or avoid him? why? How can you change that?

7. what is your prison cell? what stops you from running out into the meadow like a crazy kid? Ask God to start the process of breaking you out of prison.

Jot down a few things you don't want to forget from this chapter.

1.

2.

3.

RELENTLESS PURSUIT

Father, I want my life for you to be as fanatical as yours is for mine, so I commit to . . .

Spend a few minutes talking to God about how you feel. List some specific prayer needs and action points that will help you live out the truths in this chapter.

7

IRRESISTIBLE

The transforming tenderness for an adulteress

I was twenty years old and had never read a book from cover to cover in my life. In school I had been required to read Shakespeare's *Macbeth*, but I watched the movie instead. Now I sat on a brown vinyl beanbag with a strange little burgundy-colored book in my hand. I had been given the book at school when I was eleven years old. Nine years later its dark red cover glared at me, daring me to open it. The book was a New Testament. I didn't know much about reading books at the time, but it seemed natural to start from the beginning, so I opened at the first page and read a few lines.

I was confused. It was all about how this edition of the book had been decided and printed. I figured something wasn't quite right, so I flipped a couple of pages and tried again.

I was really confused. It was just a list of hard-to-pronounce names who "begat" and "begat" and "begat"! I figured something still wasn't quite right. I decided to give it one last chance. I flipped a few more pages and read several lines.

I was *really* confused. What I read took my breath away. I couldn't believe it was real. As I read those few pages in Matthew's Gospel I came face-to-face with a character unlike anyone I had ever encountered before. He embodied everything I had ever longed for. He seemed to overflow with genuine compassion, care and concern for people. Not just cool people who had it all together, but the awkward and undervalued, those who lacked confidence in themselves and had been shoved aside. He related to the slightly insecure and confused, the self-conscious who felt a bit overwhelmed by life and struggled with feelings that they had let their families down and amounted to nothing. In short, people just like me. No one seemed like an annoyance or nuisance. Everyone loved hanging out with this guy. More incredible to me was that he loved being with them, even if the world didn't see them as valuable.

I had never encountered anyone quite like him. I was captivated.

I felt a rush of fearful hope. Perhaps this guy would have wanted even me around? I don't know how else to say it; I simply fell in love with this character that walked across the pages of the little book. I was intoxicated. I felt like this was a man who not only knew what hurt but also knew how to heal. His gentle touch and loving acceptance enthralled me. His name was Jesus.

Then I began to notice what Jesus was saying. As I read Matthew 5–7 (the Sermon on the Mount), his words struck the very core of my heart as truth. Not just true, not just factually correct—but life-giving, freeing, soul-filling truth. What he said was not only right, it was good. I remember closing the book and thinking with amazement, *I had no idea this was in here. Why didn't anyone tell me?* I had thought the Bible was just a bunch of ancient, irrelevant fables about grumpy old people who lived a long time ago and shouted a lot. I was overwhelmed by Jesus and wanted to be around him.

I still do.

Even today when I read the Gospels, I see people drawn to Jesus, recklessly trusting him not to ignore, cast aside, judge or make fun of them. You know what? He never lets anyone down. In fact, Jesus throws his arms open wide and pleads with people to come, throw all their eggs into one basket and trust him. Jesus is simply amazing. I still find him enthralling, fascinating and compelling. He is gentle, generous, accepting and loving. He is the sort of guy that you just want to hang out with. It doesn't matter whether he is doing something or nothing—you just want to be with him. He's fun.

When I read the New Testament, I see accounts of a blind man who continued to scream at the top of his lungs for Jesus, even though those around tried to stifle him and told him he was not worth the Master's time. I read of little children who rushed into his arms as if he were their own daddy who had been away on a long trip. I see social outcasts, prostitutes, adulterers, crooked businessmen—all pushing and shoving to get close to Jesus. One man's desperation drove him up a tree! They didn't care what others would think or say; they simply wanted to touch him. Jesus didn't care what others would say either. He just wanted to be touched. Most of all, I see people like you and me.

I see people who are not superstars, not the social elite but regular, everyday people who are a little bruised, a little chipped and frayed around the edges.

In his book *What's So Amazing About Grace?* Philip Yancey wonders why it is that the sorts of people who used to flock, push and shove to be with Jesus now avoid churches like they avoid the plague. I wonder too. Jesus was the friend of the hurting and marginalized. They enjoyed his company. What was it about him?

It's very early in the morning, just before sunrise. Your eyes flutter open. You feel the hard bed underneath you. The mattress is so thin; it is little more than a padded mat sitting on top of a stiff, wooden bed frame. You wrap your arms around yourself as you sit huddled on the edge of the bed in the chilly morning air and scratch your thicket of bed head. After staring vacantly at the walls for a few minutes, you muster all your strength, stand up and get dressed. You make your way over to the window and push open the simple wooden shutters.

On the horizon you can see ribbons of dark orange sunlight outlining the distant eastern hills. The gray predawn shadows await the glow of morning sun. The city stretches as far as the eye can see. The ancient sandstone buildings are all different heights, leaning up against one another like drunks staggering home on a Friday night. Dusty narrow alleyways snake their way between the lopsided buildings.

You go down the stone stairs outside the bedroom door and find yourself standing in the dusty street below. You pass a shopkeeper beginning to set his stall out in front of his shop. He pushes up the fence that covers the windows, but he is in no hurry as it is still early. A very round, middle-aged lady ferociously slops a mop over a set of gleaming marble steps that lead up to an important building. You stop dead in your tracks. Your mouth waters as you inhale the delicious smell of freshly baked bread. Passing behind you a delivery boy pushes a cart piled high with warm loaves. Finally the street opens out into a large marketplace. On the street corner sits a newspaper stall. A couple of guys stand there and discuss the morning headlines. They agonize over the final score of the big game the night before, and comment on the government's latest policy for peace in the Middle East. The marketplace is quiet; it's still too early for the stalls to be open.

On the far side of the market, slightly down a gentle slope, a small crowd gathers and mills around. You join the crowd and make your way toward a massive stone staircase that seems to ascend to the sky before you. The group trudges up the stairs that run up the outside of a formidable sandstone wall. At the top you turn to your right and face an imposing, breathtakingly beautiful archway. Flowing script is carved around the edge of the arch. A weaving vine laden with huge bunches of grapes entwines itself around the lettering, bordered by ornately carved pomegranates, figs and other fruits. As you pass through the arch, you trace your hand over the magnificent craftsmanship. You could almost pluck the fruit and eat it.

Through the archway, a perfectly flat, sandy courtyard stretches out. The courtyard is bordered on all sides by colonnades of whitewashed columns. Streams of sunlight pour between the columns, penetrating the courtyard like arrows. Morning haze, yet to burn off in the heat of day, dances in the shafts. You take a few steps across the courtyard and stand in quiet awe. There before you, towering into the sky, is a gleaming white building. The top of the impressive structure is outlined with a band of pure gold that flashes blindingly in the morning sun. Two heavy, imposing, gold-covered doors stand slightly ajar. The doors are richly carved with fruit similar to that on the archway. On either side of the doorway are massive stone columns.

The vision is spectacular; surely this is the place where God dwells. You stand in awe of his temple.

But you are not really here for the temple this morning. Turning aside, you make your way over to a few steps in a sunbathed corner. The temple courtyard is busy yet worshipful, as devout seekers come to offer their morning prayers. In the corner a few guys—your friends—gather on the steps. You catch up on the morning news. The atmosphere is lighthearted and jovial between everyone as you sit enjoying the warm morning sun and the company of one of the rabbis.

The low hum of the priest singing psalms is suddenly punctuated by a strange yelping noise, the sort of noise a dog might make when someone stands on its tail. Everyone in the temple stops and looks up. At first you imagine it's one of the market vendors shouting in dispute over a price, but it's too early for them to be open. The noise ricochets around the colonnades, making its source hard to pinpoint. Then it stops. Slowly you go back to your conversation, but—there it is again! Where is that noise coming from, and what on earth is it anyway? It sounds like some poor animal being beaten to within an inch of its life. Again you try to shake the disturbance and go back to your conversation.

Suddenly you hear the angry shouts of an argument. Everyone in the courtyard looks around to see what the problem is, but there is nothing. The shouts are loud and vehement, yet distant. Now there is that shrieking again, followed by the shouting, which seems to be getting closer and closer. What on earth is going on? People look disapprovingly at one another, shaking their heads and muttering under their breaths.

This is supposed to be a place of worship and reverence, not a three-ring circus.

Once more you try to return to your conversation. Someone in the group thrusts his hand past your face and points back to the archway. "Look!" he shouts. You follow his finger and gaze over to the archway you entered through just a few minutes before.

The crowd of orderly people filing along underneath the arch is shoved aside as a group of men push through. People stumble, fall forward and are smashed face-first into the arch as the disorderly mob shoves and spills into the courtyard. The unruly gang stops just inside the courtyard and continues arguing, shouting at the top of their lungs. The language is unbelievable; this is a holy place, after all. And there is that strange screeching again!

You and your friends stare in utter disbelief. Then it slowly dawns on you that you recognize those guys. One of the members of your group points and says, "I know that guy—he's one of the leaders of our temple. That one is one of the teachers."

"Wait a minute—that other man is one of the leaders at *my* synagogue," someone else agrees. It's true. All these men are highly respected religious leaders known as Pharisees. They lurch and shuffle forward awkwardly as if the gang is trying to goad an unwilling donkey along in their midst. Then, without warning they stop again and start to argue, shaking their fists and kicking the dust at one another. And still, there is that strange yelping noise.

As you sit and watch the commotion, you begin to feel a little uneasy. For some unknown reason, the mob seems to be getting closer and closer to your group. People begin to stare as if you are all in some way connected to this outrageous display. The horde stops right in front of you. Suddenly, as if on cue, the group parts, revealing the dangerous animal in their midst. Jaws drop as you all stand and look in utter disbelief.

The wild, ferocious animal is . . . a woman.

She is half-naked, draped primarily in the sheet snatched from her bed, and it's not covering her very well. Her hair is frantic, one side plastered down while the other stands up straight. Her arms and legs are covered in bruises where the men have held her tightly as she struggled to get free. Her face is a deep red, a mix of ferocious anger and true shame. The woman's cheeks are flushed and wet with tears. She hangs her head, afraid to lift it up and face her accusers. The men thrust her forward for all to see.

"This woman was caught in adultery!"

Shock jolts the crowd into silence.

This whole scene is a pathetic sham—a setup to discredit Jesus, the rabbi you and your friends have gathered with. This is not about justice. It's about revenge. These Pharisees and teachers of the religious law don't like Jesus. They don't like what he says about God. It messes with their carefully organized systems of control. They had vowed that they would discredit this Jesus and show him up for the fraud they were certain he was.

In fact, just the day before, these same religious leaders had come to Jesus in the marketplace and tried to catch him out with some tricky theology. Jesus had turned the question back on them. Fueled by resentment and fear, they had stayed up all night hatching a plan that would expose this charlatan, this Jesus—for the glory of God! This time their plan came at the expense of one of God's creatures. But they didn't care about the woman. Her feelings were irrelevant. This woman was a sinner who wasn't worthy of the grace of God. She was simply a pawn to be used to make a point.

It is an obvious trap. How do fine, upstanding religious leaders just happen to stumble upon adultery while it is in progress? When was the last time you just managed to saunter in on an adulterous relationship in the heat of passion? The timing here is too convenient.

Then there is the problem of the missing man. The last time I checked, this sort of thing required two people. Why didn't these guys bring the partner in crime? The law certainly required that both offenders be brought to justice. Most of all, why bring this woman to the temple? If these leaders were concerned with the law, why not take her to the judges? Why bring her to Jesus? He has no judicial authority. He is not a judge. He's simply a traveling preacher.

The trap is set. The air is charged with expectation. The crowd holds its breath, waiting for Jesus to respond.

Often people reacted to Jesus by bowing or falling on their knees before him, but in this instance, Jesus is the one who falls to his knees. He crouches on the ground, turns his head away from the whole sorry fiasco and begins to scratch around in the dirt. I don't think Jesus is writing anything in particular on the ground, he is simply so embarrassed by this whole scene that he looks down and writes in the ground, wishing he were somewhere else. His heart is so heavy. Are these the actions of men who claim to love God? The woman's face is covered in shame, rejection and hurt. By turning away, Jesus brings some dignity to an undignified moment.

But the Pharisees aren't going to let him off the hook as easily as that. As their hands clutch stones in readiness for the punishment that must certainly be given to this woman, the leaders push Jesus to say something in response. Finally, Jesus replies. He lightly dusts off his hands as he rises, and says,

---

"OK, whoever is without sin throw the first stone."

Again he stoops down. He can hear the feet shuffling as the Pharisees turn to one another in agitation. He can hear the strain in their voices as they begin to argue and accuse one another in hushed tones, "Whose idea was this anyway?"

The crowd begins to point and murmur. Finally, with a look of pure disgust and agitation, one of the Pharisees throws his rock on the ground. The rock sends up a little puff of dust. Then he turns and pushes his way through the heckling crowd. Another rock thumps to the ground, then another and another as the Pharisees each retreat in irritation. At last everything is quiet.

It was quiet for a long time. Jesus started, like a man snapping out of a daydream. He looked up. Squinting in the climbing sun, he shaded his eyes. Everyone had gone. But wait. Not everyone.

One person was left standing before Jesus. The woman.

Why on earth was she still standing there? She had been struggling to get free from the moment she was snatched from her bed. Why, now, didn't she run away? Was she in shock? Was she so afraid that she dared not move? Or was it that she saw something in the eyes of Jesus that rooted her to the spot? Did she experience something in his voice, in his action, that drew her so strongly that she did not want to leave?

"Where is everyone? Does no one condemn you? I don't," Jesus said softly. Then as he stood up and dusted himself off, he said the most amazing thing.

"You know, you don't have to live like that anymore."

Wait a minute! What's that all about? What a thing to say! Why doesn't he witness to her, share the Bible message, lead her in a sinner's prayer or something? He doesn't even invite her to a prayer group or Bible study. This is the perfect time to share the message of God's love with her, a captive audience, and Jesus skips it! In fact, Jesus often didn't do what we might expect. The disciples didn't even get it. They'd see people come to him for help, and Jesus would say things like "Go home," "Why are you asking me?" or "Shush, don't tell anyone." Why didn't he seize the opportunity to preach them a sermon or convince them to be baptized?

Not only did he bypass the chance to talk to this woman about God, he left out something else. There was one person at that time who was qualified to judge the woman. In fact, the person just happened to be in Jerusalem that very day. He had been standing right there, among the crowd. Jesus was the only person without sin who could have rightly thrown the first stone. He was uniquely qualified to judge that woman and condemn her. His character brings our lack to the surface and exposes our shortcomings.

But he did not take the woman aside and say "Now then, let's look at your life choices up to this point. Not very clever are they? What were you thinking?" He did not point out to her how lucky she was that the Pharisees had brought her to him. He didn't hold it over her or try to emotionally blackmail her. He did not make her feel uncomfortable or spread the disappointment nice and thick. He didn't say "Well, you are going to have to show me something pretty spectacular now. I am very disappointed in you. It's going to take a lot to earn back my trust." He did not abuse her emotionally or make her feel indebted. He just freely, willingly, joyfully forgave. It's amazing—he didn't even ask her if she was sorry! He forgave her before she said she was.

---

jesus forgives with a revolutionary grace.

Why didn't Jesus share a sermon with her or invite her to an evangelistic meeting? I believe that in that moment, she had an encounter with the relentless tenderness and mercy of Jesus. What else did she need? Words were not necessary. In the eyes of Jesus of Nazareth she saw the revolution of grace, the tenderness of the tremendous lover who knows not only what hurts us but also how to heal us. There was nothing else to say—the revolution had begun.

But this isn't just a story about a woman; it is a story about me as I find myself trapped in patterns of shame and guilt from which I can find no escape, no hope. And it isn't just a story about me; it's a story about the Father's heart. Perhaps you feel like me from time to time. You are caught in bad habits, and you think your life is never going to change. You do well for a while, but sooner or later the old habit pops back up, leaving you feeling that nothing is ever going to get better. You think you have gone too far and can never receive complete forgiveness. Then you look up, and your accusers are gone. And there Jesus stands, arms open wide—irresistible. And ready to offer the transforming tenderness that will begin the revolution of grace.

OBSESSIVE BEHAVIOR

1. How would you describe Jesus to someone who knew nothing about him? What does your description of Jesus say about your relationship with him?

2. What sort of people do you attract? Why? How can we be more attractive to a lost and hurting world?

3. How do you think Jesus would do youth group or church services? Why?

4. Have you ever been emotionally blackmailed? How did it make you feel?

5. Has anyone ever told you that you need to prove yourself to God? Do you still think that is true?

6. Why do you think Jesus didn't ask the woman if she was sorry?

7. Do you think Jesus forgives us because we repent, or do you think that we repent because we have been forgiven? What do you need to be forgiven for today?

Jot down a few things you don't want to forget from this chapter.

1.

2.

3.

RELENTLESS PURSUIT

Father, I want my life for you to be as fanatical as yours is for mine, so I commit to . . .

Spend a few minutes talking to God about how you feel. List some specific prayer needs and action points that will help you live out the truths in this chapter.

8

INDESTRUCTIBLE

The real Love of peter's best friend

Poor old Pete—the apostle Peter, that is—is often portrayed as the comic relief of the Gospel stories. He always seems to be the one who says the wrong thing at the wrong time or finds some new and unusual way to put his foot in his mouth. We usually think of him as the big, burly fisherman who acts first and asks questions later, while the rest of the apostles bite their tongues and grimace. But Peter was more than just an over-exuberant apprentice Jesus had invested three years into preparing. Whatever his faults may or may not have been, Peter was a dear, close friend of Jesus. When Jesus felt the pressure of people laughing and scorning his desire to pray for a little girl who had died, Pete was one of the few he wanted in that dark little room. When Jesus went up the Mount of Transfiguration, there were only three people he wanted with him. Peter was one of them. In his time of greatest need and difficulty in the Garden of Gethsemane, Peter was one of the guys Jesus leaned upon for understanding and support.

I think there were times when Jesus looked up at the sky and thought, *What in the world is going on?* There were times when he felt misunderstood, unappreciated, lost and alone; times when he needed a confidant to share his frustrations and inner questions with; times when he just needed a friend to be there for him without challenging or questioning his every move—someone with whom he could let down his guard and just be himself. I think there were times when Jesus needed to unload the overwhelming weight he carried, to be open about his dreams and desires, to talk about the pains of being rejected and misunderstood, to be intimate and vulnerable.

Every time Jesus needed a friend, he turned to Pete. He trusted his feelings to Peter. He relied on this relationship to relax and restore.

---

peter was more than a disciple; he was one of jesus' best friends in the entire world.

Usually such close friends have a similar sense of humor, and I think Jesus and Pete did. I picture the little band of disciples trudging down some remote dusty road on their way to the next village for an evening service; it's always Jesus and Peter who are messing around, dragging behind the group, making them late. Distracted, they would run off to skip stones across the river while the rest of the disciples huffed and puffed about falling behind schedule and being late for the evening meeting. Later that night as they lay around the campfire trying to sleep, Jesus and Peter would be the ones who wouldn't stop talking. Annoyed, someone would throw pebbles at their sleeping bags and shout at them to shut up. Pete fit into that very special category—best friend.

Now Peter is collapsed on his knees, cowering in the murky corner of a dank alleyway. He hides in the shadows, desperately wishing the darkness would swallow him and his crushing guilt and shame.

How could he have done such a thing to his friend, his Lord?

He weeps and wails, crying out in anguish. Doubling over, he leans his hands against the wall and thumps his forehead on the rough sandstone. Tears stream down his face into his waterlogged beard. He has just abandoned the only one who ever really believed in him, the only one who looked past his rough exterior and saw something inside him that no one else could see. How could he have done such a thing to the only true friend he had ever really known? How could he have smashed such a precious thing as Jesus' freely given trust? Peter has just betrayed his friend and is consumed with guilt and emptiness. Now he will be condemned with his pain forever.

He has just heard the news—Jesus is dead!

He misses his friend desperately. He is overwhelmed with sorrow. If only he could turn back the clock just a few hours, he would do everything differently. He prays and pleads for the chance to go back, to be able to say it all again. But he can't . . .

Peter roams the wastelands of despair as he simultaneously roams the back alleyways of Jerusalem. He staggers along in a daze throughout the long, cold, desert night. He just walks and walks, afraid to go back, ashamed to show his face. Days later the guilt and shame are still crushing. He feels empty and numb, unworthy of life. Each breath he takes feels more pointless than the last. He slumps in the upper room, pushing his breakfast around. Who can think of eating? Peter has no appetite, no desire, no hope.

Suddenly, the door bangs open. The disciples jump to their feet, then recoil with the fear that the Sanhedrin guards have finally found their hiding place. Peter does not even flinch. Sounds seem distant to him, as if he is there but not there.

But it isn't a raid; it is Mary. She rushes into the room, her eyes bugged so wide they could have popped out of her skull. Her head scarf, normally so neat and proper, had been blown back and is now trailing along the ground behind her. Her exposed hair is windswept and bedraggled. Sweat trickles down her flushed face.

She shoots into the room like a bullet and begins ricocheting around, grabbing at the men's robes and screaming indecipherable babble. The disciples are uninterested in her foolish frenzy and swat her away. Unperturbed, Mary moves on to the next disciple, tugging and shouting. She charges around, knocking over chairs and sending a water jug crashing to the ground. A whole basket of fresh figs would have followed, but for the quick reaction of Matthew. None of the chaos she is creating seems to calm Mary down. She gets within inches of Peter who repels her with a scowl. Whatever is going on, he's not in the mood.

Nathanael grabs Mary by the shoulders and shakes her. "Calm down, woman, calm down! Take a breath! What's going on?" Mary's chest heaves as she desperately tries to catch her breath.

---

she takes two deep gulps and blurts out, "He's gone!"

Peter jumps to his feet and hits the door seconds before John, who has to pull up for fear of being thrust into the doorframe by the juggernaut fisherman. They barrel down the stairs, skipping three or four at a time. John stays close behind Pete. As they leave the house, they can still hear Mary's voice screeching from the room, "Something's happened! Something's happened!"

Peter leaps the last few stairs and lands in the crowded street below without skipping a beat. The street is jammed with carts and stalls piled high with melons, figs, rugs and clay pots in a myriad of shapes, sizes and colors. Shopkeepers shout over one another in their thunderous voices, "Fresh figs! Get ya fresh fi-igs!"

A crowd of children squeal with delight as a monkey, dressed in a little red waistcoat and purple fez, flips over and over while his master grinds out a tune. The street is thronged with people from distant countries wearing unusual headdresses and brightly colored robes. Peter pushes through the market crowds, squeezing between the animated bargain hunters.

Finally he turns the corner into an open street. His mind is reeling as he takes off running through the outskirts of Jerusalem. He doesn't know what to think or feel because his whole body seems to be swirling with thoughts and feelings. He flashes through the outer gates of the city into the forest of olive trees that line the hillsides beyond the city walls. It is hard to control his stride, and his arms flail in the air as he lurches down the hill into the garden beyond. Racing along a path that snakes between freshly turned flower beds, he can see the tomb a little farther down the slope beyond the hedgerow. The massive stone door has been rolled along its channel to one side, exposing the small square opening behind it.

Pete is within a few feet when suddenly he freezes. He is afraid to take another step, afraid that Mary might be right.

Finally he ducks into the cavity and disappears into the darkness. It takes a second for his eyes to adjust from the bright sunshine outside. He glances around the tomb, but it is empty.

Peter's heart sinks. Emotions overwhelm him—confusion, frustration. Then he begins to panic. Everything is spiraling out of control. His head spins too, as he staggers back into the bright daylight.

He stumbles over to the two guards who sit on a wall, unwrapping their sandwiches. Peter flings out his arm, backhanding the sandwich right out of one soldier's grasp. The guard glances up in confusion and anger, but before he can respond, Peter grabs him and begins to shake him. The other guard tries to pull the madman off his partner, but it is as if Pete is possessed with the strength of Samson. He screams, demanding to know what they have done with the body. The guards protest that they don't know anything, that he is crazy. But they are the guards—they have to know something. Peter lets loose a torrent of verbal abuse and then in frustration pushes the guard backwards into a thorn bush.

Sweat is pouring down Pete's angry red face as he runs back toward the city. He bursts through the doors of a city official's office, ignoring the protests of a receptionist. The bureaucrat is in the middle of a meeting and will not abide such a blatant interruption. But the self-righteous outrage on the official's face quickly turns to surprised shock as Peter barrels across the desk toward him.

slamming his fist into the desk, pete demands to know why jesus' body has been moved and where.

He shouts, rants and raves, but the official has no idea what he is talking about. According to his records, this Jesus whom Peter is shouting about had been crucified and buried just a few days before. Why would anyone move him? Peter can't control his rage. He sweeps a lamp and nameplate off the desk in his frustration, turns and storms out of the building.

The members of the Sanhedrin, the Jewish council of religious leaders, had just reconvened after the Sabbath break and were in the middle of a heated theological discussion. Peter shoves open the massive doors to the council meeting room. Every head turns. What is the meaning of this disrespect? Who dares to interrupt such an important meeting? Peter stands in the middle of the courtroom, scanning the crowd of dignified old men with their long, gray beards and fat bellies. He focuses on Caiaphas, who sits on a gold-colored chair with a luxurious red cushion. Pete thrusts his finger at the pious-looking leader and unleashes a volley of abuse. "You got rid of him—at least let him rest in peace! You've won; you got what you wanted—what more do you need? Why have you done this? That grave was given to us."

Peter vehemently accuses the Pharisees of some evil subterfuge and deceit, but they have no idea what he is talking about. They look around the room in complete confusion. They had been very careful to confirm Jesus' death and that the tomb was sealed from the outside. They are just as eager as Peter to know what is going on and where that body is. The chatter quickly escalates into a political argument about making Jesus a martyr and what rumors this could lead to. The arguing becomes so fierce that they simply forget Peter is still standing there. Peter's head sags. He turns and slowly shuffles out of the building unnoticed.

It is late that evening when he finally gives up the search and returns to the upper room. The others try to console him. They toss around some possible explanations, but no one can seriously believe what Mary is saying about Jesus actually being alive. Peter is inconsolable.

He holds his head in his hands. He had already lost his friend; now he has even lost his friend's remains.

All that is left are the feeble conspiracy theories of the other disciples and the swooning, excited ramblings of a madwoman who has obviously had way too much stress and slipped over the edge. Mary is still lost in a fairy tale of denial, running all over the city to tell everyone that Jesus is alive, *when he is obviously dead!*

But all the disciples were soon convinced that Jesus was really alive when he appeared to them in Jerusalem. He brought them peace, something they desperately needed. And then he was gone again. Perhaps the disciples thought they had seen their Lord now for the last time. In any case, they returned home to Galilee.

Afterwards Jesus appeared again to his disciples by the Sea of Galilee. It happened this way. Picking up their lives where they had left off, the disciples went back to their fishing. Their lives had turned back three years. Peter stood in the bow of the boat and looked over the smooth lake. Everything was still. He sighed, lost in another time and place as he stared into the deep, thinking. He used to be content on this lake; it was his whole world. Now it was like a prison—a constant reminder of what real life felt like. Inside, Peter died a little more every day. How could life ever be the same without his best friend?

Pete and the other guys had been fishing most of the night. All they had caught were a couple of sickly looking fish and an old wheel. The sun slowly pulled itself up from behind the Jordanian mountains. It was time to head back and clean the nets. As they rowed toward the dock, they saw the dark figure of a man walking on the beach. A dog bounded up to him. The man wrestled a stick from the dog's mouth and threw it while the dog sprinted ahead. The stranger paused, then turned to look at the boat as it drew closer.

"No luck?" he shouted. "Try throwing your nets out on the other side."

Peter swung round. Who was this idiot? Telling him, an experienced fisherman, how to fish! He was just about to give this amateur an earful, when John sprang to his feet.

The hairs stiffened on the back of his neck as he blurted out, "Jesus?"

The words had barely left John's lips before Peter jumped to his feet and began to push his way to the front of the boat. In the commotion John was sent flying backwards, landing among the nets that were piled in the back of the boat. He looked up, bemused, but Pete was long gone. Peter grabbed his robe and, slipping his arms into the sleeves, spun it above his head and down onto his back in one fluid movement. He sprang from the boat like a sprinter exploding out of the blocks. He belly flopped into the water and started flailing his arms like a madman. He swam with all of his strength, desperate to get to Jesus.

Peter had denied and deserted Jesus, but he was not afraid of him. Whatever had happened, he did not allow the past to paralyze his present response. He would not allow feelings of guilt or shame from past actions to predict and determine his future.

I often wonder what I would have done if I had been in Pete's place. What if I had denied and deserted Jesus? Would my feelings of guilt, shame and self-condemnation drive me to hide in fear, or would I try with all of my might to be with Jesus? What would you do? I think I probably would have jumped into the water. Then I would have swum the other way! I don't think I would have wanted to come face-to-face with Jesus—at least not until I could do something to prove my repentance and recommit myself. Not until I had gotten back into my Bible reading, prayer time and church attendance. I would want to wait a few days, keep my spiritual nose clean and not get into any major sin. Then I would feel better prepared to come to Jesus, tail between my legs, and recommit to living up to his expectations.

I guess I imagine that if I did swim up to shore, I would find Jesus with a very disappointed look on his face. One of those you-let-me-down-so-I'm-going-to-make-you-feel-really-bad-about-yourself looks. Peter must have known that Jesus wouldn't meet him with a guilt-inducing, disappointed stare. Peter must have known that Jesus would meet him with a radiant smile, a smile that was just happy to see him and be with him again.

---

jesus' followers were crazy about him. more amazing than that, jesus was crazy about them.

What was it about Jesus that disarmed people and drew them to him regardless of the circumstances? I think Jesus was real. By that I mean he was approachable, he was genuine. It amazes me how Jesus could move effortlessly from court to curb. He could be at a black-tie dinner in a presidential palace and feel quite at home. Then he could walk out the front door, sit down on the curb with a homeless guy and be just as comfortable. More surprising is that both types of people were just as comfortable with Jesus. Both were glad of his company and happy to hang out with him. The Bible says that crowds flocked to be with Jesus all the time. He was such a compelling guy that one time people sat with him for three days and three nights straight. No one left for lunch, no one left for dinner and no one went home to bed. For seventy-two hours people just wanted to be with him. Finally Jesus felt bad for the mob—four thousand men, plus women and children—that were hanging with him and wanted to make breakfast for them!

He was such an exciting, impulsive guy. One minute he'd be laughing and joking and the next, crying out in grief over a city. Several times Jesus cried, right out there in public in front of his manly men. He would perform an amazing miracle and then praise the other person saying, "It's your faith that has healed you."

People opened up to Jesus. He had a knack of getting right to the heart of an issue. Religious leaders of the day were called Pharisees, which means "separated," because they thought they were better than everyone else and too good to mingle with the "little people." Jesus, on the other hand, loved to be among the people. People even grabbed at his clothes, desperate to touch him. His whole ministry was a series of interruptions. Everywhere he went people sidetracked him with their needs. He didn't see them as nuisances; he saw them as opportunities. He transcended status and even race. Jesus was relational, not task-oriented, and people loved being with him.

What Jesus did would change the world and write history, yet his mission was horribly underfinanced. His people were always broke. He had to send Peter fishing to pay the bills. As he spoke to a crowded market square, he had to borrow a coin to make his illustration. Yet when he met rich, influential people, he never tried to tap them for contributions. He never pulled out a copy of his newsletter and asked if he could tell them about the work he was doing among the poor and the lepers, or about the latest short-term outreach they were raising funds for. He cared about what he could do for them, not what they could do for him.

How did Jesus manage this extraordinary life?

He genuinely loved people. He was never in a rush, he never blew people off and he never saw people as a distraction or disturbance, because he really cared about them and valued them. He recklessly threw open his heart and his arms and passionately shouted for all to come to him. Anyone who was lost, hurting, broken, ashamed, fatherless or rejected could come and find acceptance. He promised never to leave or forsake, never to abandon or reject. Jesus would never tell people to cut their hair, take out their piercings or change their styles of clothing. People were important to him. They still are.

Jesus himself said that a real friend would even give up his life for another:

"Greater love has no one than this, that he lay down his life for his friends." John 15:13

Then he did it!

Jesus loved to be surrounded by regular, everyday people. People just like me . . . people just like you . . . people who don't have it all together . . . people a little rough around the edges . . . people with a few chips and cracks . . . people a little frayed in places.

Jesus reveals a God who is not removed, not distant but approachable and intoxicating—a God who cares about us, wherever we are, wherever we've been, whatever we're doing. Not for what we can do for him but simply for who we are.

The writer of the Gospel of John often refers to the apostle John as the "disciple whom Jesus loved" (for example, see John 21:7). Do you know who wrote that book? John. Think about that. He chose to refer to himself as the "disciple whom Jesus loved." What do you think all the other apostles thought about that when it hit the local bookshops? They must have gone ballistic. What nerve! What about them—didn't Jesus love them too? How arrogant was that? Why did John give himself such a magnificent title? That's easy—it was true. He *was* the disciple whom Jesus loved.

I challenge you. Next time you meet someone new, just introduce yourself as the "disciple whom Jesus loves." See how they respond to that one. The very thought of doing that makes me want to run in fear. How could we do such an arrogant thing? Because it's true. Regardless of how you feel, you are the disciple whom Jesus loves. As Henri Nouwen says in *Life of the Beloved*, "You are the Beloved, and all I hope is that you can hear these words as spoken to you with all the tenderness and force that love can hold. My only desire is to make these words reverberate in every corner of your being—You are the Beloved." The Beloved is your true identity—the true you. It is not just a catchy thing to say in a touchy-feely book—it is the Father's name for you and the way he sees you. You may not feel like it, but it is your true identity, just as it was John's. Just as it was Peter's.

After Peter and the other disciples had eaten a breakfast of fresh fish and bread with Jesus on the shore, Jesus turned to Peter and asked, "Do you really love me more than anyone?"

"You know I do, Lord," Peter replied, without even a waver.

Jesus' eyes seemed to pierce into Peter's soul. Peter wanted to turn away, remembering the shame of his too recent betrayal of his friend and Lord. But he held Jesus' gaze as Jesus commanded, "Feed my sheep."

Feed my sheep? Jesus was entrusting his flock, his people, his followers and his friends to the care of Peter.

Jesus did not ask Peter to prove himself or earn back his trust. He did not give up on Pete and bypass him altogether. Peter's past was in the past. He must now live as Peter the apostle, Peter the shepherd, Peter the friend of Jesus.

How do you identify yourself?

Many of us stagger through life under the crushing burden of a false identity. It forces us to pretend, to hide in the corner or to shrink back when everything inside us wants to let loose with reckless abandon and just be ourselves. This false identity bullies us into the corner, keeping us afraid to let our true self out for fear of ridicule and rejection. Finally, it squeezes us into the mold of mediocrity. Our false identities can be "I'm not pretty enough . . . not thin enough . . . not popular enough . . . not talented enough . . . not smart enough . . . not cool enough." We identify ourselves as "the ones who never could quite live up to our parents' expectations or our culture's demands."

I often allow my false identity to define me. At those critical moments when I long to open up to the world, to be spontaneous and carefree, it squeezes me with its accusations and tells me that the Father's acceptance is only really for the special few, the "perfect" Christians; that things are never really going to be any different; that I will always struggle with my thoughts and disappoint God; that nobody really needs me or wants me around; that I have nothing to offer; that I am just a mistake and everything I do ends in failure; that true freedom is just wishful thinking.

---

what identity do you normally put on yourself? where did you get it? like peter and john, we need to begin to radically redefine ourselves according to our true identities in jesus.

But this is not just a story about Peter. It is a story about me, as I continue to dwell on ways I have denied Jesus. And it's not just a story about me; it's a story about the Father. It does not matter what we have done, how badly we feel we have let Jesus down or how unworthy of his love we feel. He is crazy about us. You are beloved, the disciple whom Jesus loves. The theologian Paul Tillich says, "Trust is the courage to accept acceptance." Dare to believe and allow the heavenly Father to forgive you and radically redefine your identity. You are beloved. It's how the Father defines you.

OBSESSIVE BEHAVIOR

1. put yourself in peter's place as he stood in the boat. what would you have done?

2. How do you respond to jesus when you feel like you disappoint or fail him during your daily christian life?

3. Are there areas in your life where you have allowed your past to predict or shape your future?

4. Describe how a best friend should be. Is your relationship with jesus like that? Is there anything you would be truly willing to die for? would you die for jesus?

5. Do you feel like a disciple whom jesus loves? Do you act like it? why or why not?

6. what is your identity—how do you usually think of yourself? what are some practical ways you can begin to redefine your identity?

Jot down a few things you don't want to forget from this chapter.

1.

2.

3.

RELENTLESS PURSUIT

Father, I want my life for you to be as fanatical as yours is for mine, so I commit to . . .

Spend a few minutes talking to God about how you feel. List some specific prayer needs and action points that will help you live out the truths in this chapter.

9

IMPASSIONED

The compelling mercy of Jesus for a leper

It's one of those perfect-weather days. The sun is shining, and there's not a cloud in the sky. A soft, cool breeze gently plays upon our faces, tempering the warm rays. We sit on a rolling hillside, shaded by the large spreading branches of a leafy tree. Leaning back and resting against the thick, smooth trunk, we look around to enjoy the view. Farther down the meadow, a jumbled little fishing village hugs the banks of the lake. The simple houses are clean and neat. The community has a sense of pride and small-town goodness. The village clusters around a central dockside.

As usual the quay is a hubbub of activity. Boats come and go. A group of heavily bearded men chat and joke with one another as they meticulously clean the slime from their nets. Members of a fishing crew slap one another on the back as they haul their nets, bursting with silvery fish, onto the dock to be weighed and counted. Just to the side is a long wooden workbench where young apprentices are tirelessly working at breakneck speed, gutting and cleaning the day's catch.

Beyond the village, the Sea of Galilee stretches out as far as the eye can see. The brilliant sunlight glistens and shimmers in gold strands on the gently lapping waves. From up here, the lake sparkles like a bowl of precious jewels. A couple of fishing boats bob up and down on the water as men hurl their nets into the deep. Distracted, we turn back and look around. Quite a large crowd has made its way to our picturesque hillside. Some stand under the shade of the trees, while most sit either on the dry grass or on small rocks and boulders that litter the hillside. Everyone there is focused and intently listening to a local teacher who has recently arrived in the area.

The arrival of a traveling speaker is not all that unusual; in fact, it's the time of year when they often come around conducting their revival meetings.

---

but this rabbi is different.

We have heard sermons before—truckloads of them, in fact—but when this guy speaks it's as if we are hearing truth for the first time. He speaks with such an easy grace. He is casual, almost lighthearted, as if he were just chatting away with you one-on-one over coffee, yet his words carry weight—an authority that snaps you to attention and compels you to listen up. With this guy it's not just theoretical, it's real life. It's as if his words have the force of Heaven behind them. They are amazing, strangely familiar yet shockingly new—unlike anything we have heard before. His words seem to penetrate to the very core of our being, resounding with truth.

---

what he is saying is not only true—it's good.

Our spirits soar with new hope as we listen. The crowds sit in absolute amazement at his words. But they haven't come simply to be entertained by his smooth delivery style. Word is that when this guy prays, creation itself sits up and listens. There have been rumors about miracles, healings; even evil spirits run and hide from this guy. The atmosphere is thick with expectation. All around people with crutches, bandaged limbs, wheelchairs, even guide dogs, sit anxiously waiting his call during the ministry time. Over to one side a crowd of Pharisees has gathered to supervise the service and take notes on what needs to be censored. They are huddled together, arms tightly folded in a stance of disapproval and defiance. Someone whispers that this group of Pharisees had a heated run-in with this teacher in the neighboring village just the day before. The teacher, who we have heard comes from the small working-class town of Nazareth and goes by the name of Jesus, sits on a large boulder slightly to one side of the crowd, talking about true happiness. We listen transfixed.

Once he has finished teaching, Jesus slips off the rock and dusts the dirt from his robe. Immediately, the crowd jumps to its feet and begins to press around the speaker. Everyone pushes in trying to ask questions, receive prayer or invite Jesus to their homes for lunch. A band of twelve disciples, some of them local fishermen, form a ring of protection around their master, in a futile attempt at crowd control. Jesus, who seems happy to meet and greet, is smiling, shaking hands and listening intently as people pour out their requests. As he chats Jesus begins to stroll casually down the hillside toward the small village. The throng of people moves in unison with him like a pack of swarming bees around a honeypot. Our little group looks at one another with expressions that ask, "Should we follow?" We have to make our way down to the village anyway, and besides, we are keen to see what might happen next, so we jump up and follow the herd.

Sauntering along we discuss the words we have just heard.

"Did you hear what he said about that? Wow, how do you do that? I will need to think that one over. . . ."

Eventually, buildings force the crowd to shoehorn itself into a dusty, narrow street on the outskirts of town. The crowd slows to a shuffle as people patiently wait their turns to merge with the mass entering the lane. It's like being at a concert or sports event that's just finished, with the crowd slowly meandering down the exit ramp before spilling into the parking lot. We are right at the back, but that's OK. We are feeling very charitable and pause to let a gaggle of old ladies go ahead of us.

As we join the press of people in the street, however, we begin to wonder why we are moving so slowly. What are the people in front doing? Don't they know we want to get there as well? Can't they get a move on? Then without explanation, the shuffle stops. At first we wait as patiently as we can. We turn to one another and exchange looks of bemusement. But after a minute or two, we gently prod the backs of the people in front of us. They turn around and huff, "Hey, buddy, there's nowhere to go." It's been two or three minutes since we moved at all, and now we are beginning to get a bit impatient. Again we gently shove the people in front. "What's going on? Why aren't we moving?" But they have no idea why we're stopped either, and they are just as anxious to get moving as we are.

Something is definitely wrong. We have been stopped too long. You look around for a hole in the crowd to slip through and snake your way to the front, but there's no way through; it's shoulder to shoulder. Then you notice a low wall along the side of the street. Someone gives you a leg up so you can see what's going on. Tottering slightly on the frail wall, you wobble for a moment before finding your balance. The rest of the group anxiously waits to find out if you can see anything.

Looking over the sea of bobbing heads, you can just make out the front of the crowd. You can see Jesus standing in the middle, but wait!

---

all of a sudden the calm explodes.

The crowd around Jesus erupts into a rage of shouting, pushing and screaming. Pandemonium breaks out. People shove one another in anger; some throw fists and elbows. Some of the guys turn around to those behind them, kicking up the dust with their feet and spitting at one another. Then everyone pulls away, giving Jesus wide berth. They fight to get away from him. People are pushing and shoving so violently that one man is knocked down and trampled underfoot. Just a minute ago these same people were crowding to get close to Jesus; now it is every man for himself to get away. No one is within six feet of the sought-after speaker. The crowd heaves and sways as the people behind push in and the people at the front fight to push back. It looks like a schoolyard fight as the gang circles up around the action.

And there Jesus is, a lone figure in the middle of the circle. It is amazing. He isn't reacting to what is going on around him at all. He doesn't even seem to notice. He's just standing there, alone.

Hang on—he's not alone.

A man stands in the circle with him. The man's robe reaches all the way to the ground. His head is bowed low and his hood is up; he looks like a mysterious Jedi knight. He is holding a well-worn staff and is barefoot. His other hand is tucked behind his back. His robe is ratty, threadbare and frayed. There are grass stains, dust and dirt ground into one side from sleeping outside every night. One of the sleeves has food stains on it where he rummaged through a dumpster looking for scraps to eat. He looks like he has been homeless for decades. Then you see the arm that had been hidden fall to his side. He's holding a small bell on the end of an old piece of rope.

Wow, this guy isn't just homeless—he has leprosy!

Leprosy was the most horrific, feared disease of Jesus' day. It was an excruciatingly painful one in which your body seemed literally to rot to death. To the people of that time, lepers were stinking, walking corpses. Their bodies were covered in open sores that wept and bled. In advanced cases, the disease damaged nerves to such an extent that infections could set in before the sufferer noticed. Parts of the body eventually decayed completely, leaving huge wounds and deformed body parts.

The disease was shrouded in mystery. No one knew how it was transmitted. There was no cure. Along with the terrible physical discomfort, there was the social stigma. Leprosy was such a vile, painful, horrible, slow death that people assumed it was the curse of God. If you had leprosy, you must be such a depraved sinner that even God would not have mercy upon you. Leprosy was the curse of sinful actions. To imagine the response to leprosy in the religiously charged atmosphere of Jesus' day, think of many people's response to AIDS. How do they react to it? They immediately reject the afflicted person and pull away, afraid that somehow the curse might be transmitted to them. Their minds whirl and race as they think, *what has that person been up to, where have they been?* Some feel no remorse for those suffering, believing it to be God's punishment for sinful living.

People with leprosy were the rejects of society. In fact in society's eyes, a leper was considered dead. Funeral rites were said over them, and they basically ceased to exist. They were dead to family, friends, career, hopes, dreams and future. Victims of leprosy were banished from the city, forced to live the remainder of their lives beyond the city walls. It was such a feared, agonizing disease that no one wanted even to have to look at its sufferers—they were beyond help, and definitely must be beyond God's forgiveness.

But this guy was just like you or me. In fact, it could have been me; it could have been you.

This decrepit old tramp surely hadn't always had leprosy; there may have been a time when he was just a regular Joe. Perhaps he was a young man, with a beautiful young wife and a couple of little kids. He could have had a house with a white picket fence, a career and plans for the family's first summer vacation to Disneyland. He may have dreamed of the future, of seeing his kids' first ball games, dance recitals, even one day his own grandkids. He probably had the same dreams we have.

It was early one Saturday morning when he woke. Yawning, he rolled over to look at the alarm clock and rubbed the sleep out of his eyes. As he pulled his hand away, he noticed a blemish on the back of it. He felt the tense grip of anxiety grab his spine. His heart beat a little faster as he sat upright in bed and began to rub the back of his hand. The blemish seemed to be under the skin. He licked his fingers and vigorously rubbed the mark with his spit. Nothing changed. He shoved his elbow into his wife's ribs to get her attention.

"Leave me alone; it's too early," she replied sleepily.

"Wake up," he whispered as he shook her shoulder.

"It's your turn to check on the kids. Give me five more minutes to sleep," she grumbled.

Again he jammed his bony elbow into her ribs and insisted she turn around. A deep furrow on her brow announced her displeasure at being disturbed. She fought to open one eyelid and looked up from the pillow. He thrust his hand under her bleary eye. Shrieking, she sat bolt upright in bed.

"what is that? where did you get it . . . where have you been . . . what have you been doing?"

Suddenly the air was charged with tense accusations. His pulse raced, and the hairs on the back of his neck stood up straight. "What do you mean? I haven't been anywhere! What is this?"

Hunched over, they both rubbed and picked at the blemish. They emptied the medicine cabinet in the bathroom and smeared every ointment they had on his hand, but nothing made any difference. His wife ran into the bedroom, grabbed his robe and threw it at him. "Quickly, go to the doctor!"

While he sat in the waiting room, his mind was racing as he mentally retraced his every step to account for the inexplicable. His heart thumped in his chest. He wracked his brain to think where he could have come into contact with anything unusual.

Finally he was called into the examination room. In this man's day the doctor was the local priest. His hand trembled slightly as he extended it toward the priest. "This is nothing, right? You can give me something to clear this up, can't you? I'm sure it's nothing serious. . . ."

"Wait a moment," replied the priest as he poured a little oil onto the blemish.

The priest shuffled to the back of the room and began whispering with one of the other priests. *What was taking so long? This couldn't be good.* The young man started to get very nervous at the lack of assurance.

"I'm sure it's nothing," he stammered, "I can come back some other time."

He stood up to make his getaway, but the priest stood in front of him and insisted he sit. He could feel beads of sweat roll down his back as he waited. A knot pulled tight in his stomach. The priest held a candle over the blemish, and then with sad eyes he lowered his head.

"I'm sorry, son; you have . . . you have the plague."

The young man jumped to his feet, kicking and screaming, "No! No, you're wrong! I don't have leprosy; I can't have leprosy. I'm a good person; I'm not bad. I want a second opinion. What do *you* know? You're wrong!"

As he shouted he tried to push the priest out of the way, but two larger priests blocked the door. They grabbed him firmly by the shoulders and dragged him screaming and squirming back to the chair. As the man fought desperately to escape, they pinned him down and tore the clothes from his back. They stripped him naked and threw his robes onto the fire for fear that they had been contaminated. Then they began to ritually wash and cleanse him.

He screamed to be released. He shouted for his rights, but he no longer had any rights.

The priest explained that he had no rights, no life, no future. His old life was dead.

He could never go back to it. The man kicked and flayed about in desperation but could not break free. He cried out for help, but none came. Nearing exhaustion, he fell to his knees and began to negotiate. If they would just let him go, just pretend that he had never been there . . . In despair he grabbed the sandaled feet of the priest and, with his lips touching the rough toes, begged permission to go home one last time. He had left in such a rush, there was so much he wanted to say, so much that was left undone. If only he could go home and hold his wife one last time. To sit his kids on his knees and tell them how much their daddy loved them. To assure them that it wasn't their fault. That he would always remember them, always be thinking of them—always love them.

But he could never go home.

Never again would he know the touch of human acceptance.

For the rest of his pain-filled life, he had to avoid every human contact. By law he had to leave the city immediately and never return. He was given an old robe, a staff and a bell. If anyone even came close to him he had to ring the bell and shout out, "I am unclean!" Not sick or unwell—unclean. How long would you have to shout out that destiny before you began to believe it?

How long until you began to think, *Perhaps I am unclean. Perhaps there is something wrong with me. Perhaps I am a bad person unworthy of the Father's mercy.* Would it take a week, a month, a year, five years, ten years, twenty years?

Added to his sentence was the certain knowledge that his family would be branded and rejected. They wouldn't be welcome in temple meetings. They would have to sit alone, while all the other women whispered and pointed, "Have you heard about her husband? What sort of sin goes on in their house?" The kids would come home from school in tears from the others teasing them for being "leper kids." They wouldn't want to go to school anymore. The family would be forced to beg and rely on the charity of extended family members in order to eat. In their society women could not earn a living, and so they would be destitute. The pain, rejection, frustration, confusion and heartache would haunt this young man for the rest of his life. He was cursed. There was no escape from his misery.

Many years later, he found himself at the end of his rope. He just couldn't go on like this one day longer. He was desperate for release from his anguish. Then when he thought all hope was lost, he heard about a man who was different from all the others. This was a rabbi who spoke soothing words that felt like a cool balm, a teacher who accepted the downcasts and outcasts with grace and made even the rejected feel welcome and special. He heard a rumor that this rabbi would pray for the sick and forgotten and that many were completely healed.

---

jesus was this man's last hope.

He had to get to Jesus. He broke the law and walked into the outskirts of the town. Without care for the law, he walked up to the crowd. What did it matter to him? They couldn't punish him any more than they had. He was already dead. He began to push his way through the crowd, desperate to get to Jesus.

At first no one noticed. They thought it was just another person in the crowd pushing and shoving. People shoved back, "Hey, buddy, wait your turn; we all want to get there." Then someone turned and saw the puss-filled sores on his face and screamed,

"*Leper!*" Immediately the crowd fought to get away. They began to beat the man with their staffs, desperate to drive him away. They cursed at him and scorned him, shaking their fists in righteous anger. How dare he defile this place? The people kept pushing to get away and the man kept pushing his way through until finally, he found himself standing face-to-face with Jesus.

Now from your perch on the wall, you can see the crowd heaving and swaying as they scream and shout their abuse and rejection. Someone in the crowd has thrown a stone. It pelts the leprous man in his temple, and blood trickles down the side of his beard. Another stone thumps into his shoulder, and another and another. The crowd roars with disdain as the man remains motionless, his head bowed in shame and fear. As he stands in front of Jesus, all of the pain, frustration, rejection and heartache begin to well up within him. His hands start to tremble, then his shoulders, until finally he erupts like a volcano. A torrent of pain flows uncontrollably. He screams in agony as he weeps and weeps. The crowd barely hears his cries over their uproar. He cries so much and so hard that eventually his knees buckle and he crashes to the ground in front of Jesus—a crumpled mass of humanity. He bows in shame as years of misery pour out. He gulps the air and splutters his plea,

---

"If . . . if you are willing . . . if you are willing, you can make me clean."

There are times in Scripture when people came to Jesus in need of healing, and he simply said the word and they were healed. There was a time when Jesus healed a servant without even having to visit him. He told the master to go home; and when the master arrived home, he found his servant was completely better. There was even a time when Jesus gave a group discount to ten men with leprosy. Without batting an eye, Jesus told them to go show themselves to the doctor, and on their way they were totally healed.

Jesus could have said the word of healing to this man, and it would have been so. But Jesus had something better in mind. As he looked at the man and saw his need and deep feelings of rejection, worthlessness and shame, he was overcome with compassion.

The world Jesus lived in was influenced by Greece. The Greeks taught that God had no emotion. They reasoned that if you could make God happy or sad, then you would have control over him and thus be greater than he was. For God to be supreme he must be above all, moved by nothing. *Compassion* means that you are moved to the depths of your being. To the Greeks, it was impossible for God to be moved in such a way. Yet every time the word *compassion* is used in the New Testament, it is in reference to Jesus.

Jesus enters into the deepest feelings of pain, loneliness, shame, despair or joy and experiences them in their entirety with us. He feels the limp of those who are crippled and the loneliness of those who are rejected. Jesus reveals a Father who is not removed and untouchable but who is moved to the very depths of his being by our need and struggle.

Now, the man with leprosy is hunched over in front of Jesus. Jesus is so overwhelmed with compassion for this chipped and cracked vessel that, without saying a word, he too falls to his knees in the middle of the dusty lane. He leans over and tenderly takes the man by the shoulder. Very gently he begins to lift the man's trembling shoulders. At first the man resists. He buries his face into Jesus' chest, too ashamed to have this strange rabbi look at him and see his oozing sores.

---

jesus reaches out his hand and slowly lifts the man's head.

He examines the open wounds and the face covered with fear and shame. Awed by such grace, the man tries to divert his eyes, but he can't escape the all-encompassing gaze of acceptance and care. Tears stream down his scarred and hurting face.

Without a word, Jesus slides his hands from the man's face down to his shoulders. Jesus throws his arms around this outcast and gives him a huge bear hug! How long has it been since this man knew the touch of human acceptance? Jesus doesn't seem to care about the open sores, the smell of rotting flesh, the fear of transmission or of becoming unclean.

The crowd is in shock. Dumbfounded with horror, they have fallen silent. They just stand there staring as the two men embrace in the middle of the street.

Even from this distance you can tell that Jesus is whispering something into the man's ear. As the man reveals later, Jesus is saying, "It's not your fault. The Father doesn't hate you; he loves you. He has been searching the barren places, longing to find you and bring you home. You are not cursed or forsaken."

---

jesus pulls away from the man slightly, and looking at the crowd, he speaks for all to hear, "of course I am willing!"

Jesus rises to his feet, and as he does so, he lifts the man to his. Get this—the guy's not diseased anymore. His skin is completely pure! The man can hardly suppress his excitement. He falls back down in front of Jesus. Some in the crowd hang their heads in shame for having judged so harshly; others are waving their hands in disgust and walking away. One thing you realize as you process this incredible sight—that man has been healed of a lot more than leprosy.

But this isn't just a story about a leper; it is a story about me as I feel I am on the outside looking in. And it isn't just a story about me; it's a story about the Father's heart.

If you are anything like me, there are probably times when you feel like the man with leprosy: estranged, different, beyond mercy or hope, consumed with feelings that it is too late for you, that the gulf is too wide or that you are on the outside looking in.

You live on the fringes, desperately wishing you could somehow be closer. Perhaps you are consumed with feelings that you're unclean or unworthy. Most of the time I pretend that everything is fine, while inside I wonder what it is about me that banishes me to the outskirts. I look longingly at other people's talents, gifts or abilities. I wonder why they have such a strong calling while I fumble around, desperate to do something for God but unsure what that is. I struggle to find intimacy in worship. Finally I resign myself to second-class citizenship and stand awkwardly and insecurely over by the wall while the cool kids enter in. If you know what I am talking about, the Father longs to kneel with you, throw his arms around you and love the pain away. He is more than willing.

The night before his death, Jesus sat in the upper room with his disciples and shared the Father's heart with them. After some time a slightly agitated Philip cut Jesus off in mid-sentence and, throwing his arms up in frustration, blurted out, "Jesus, just show us the Father and it will be enough."

I think Jesus probably had tears in his eyes as he looked at Philip and said quietly, "Oh, Phil, after three years have you not seen any of the Father in me?"

"Anyone who has seen me has seen the Father." John 14:9

If we want to know what God is like, we have to look at Jesus, because he said that to see him is to see the Father. What is the Father's heart like? It is transforming tenderness that freely forgives and restores; it is love that is real, approachable and accepting, even if we have denied and deserted him; it is compassion that heals our deepest wounds and unseemliness.

As you read this you may be feeling a little like Phil, struggling to catch a glimpse of God's glory through a fog of uncertainty and doubt. Perhaps you are not sure about this revelation of God's tender, real, compassionate heart. You may not be sure you can believe that the character of Jesus is that of the Father. Old images hold you back, and you wonder which can be trusted. Jesuit theologian Karl Rahner said, "Jesus is the human face of God." God knows no season of change. He has one unchanging, unmovable stance towards us—he passionately loves us. Dare to trust him; dare to believe.

OBSESSIVE BEHAVIOR

1. Are there times when you feel like the man with leprosy—on the fringes, on the outside looking in? What has caused those feelings? Where did they come from?

2. What lies have been spoken about you that you have begun to identify with over time? Will you bring them to Jesus and let Him speak truth about you instead?

3. Have you ever thought that your actions have an effect on the Father? How does that make you feel? How does it change your perception of God?

4. In the past, have you thought of the Father's characteristics and Jesus' characteristics as different? Why?

5. Think about Jesus' words that to see Him is to see the Father. What do you think about that? What should you do to understand God more?

6. People often tried to arrest Jesus, but the Bible says, "His time had not yet come" (John 7:30). What do you think was the main purpose for Jesus' three years of public life?

jot down a few things you don't want to forget from this chapter.

1.

2.

3.

RELENTLESS PURSUIT

Father, I want my life for you to be as fanatical as yours is for mine, so I commit to . . .

Spend a few minutes talking to God about how you feel. List some specific prayer needs and action points that will help you live out the truths in this chapter.

10

INEXPLAINABLE

The mysterious journey of Noah

God is often described with long, sterile, theological words like *omniscient*, *omnipotent*, *immutable* or *sovereign*, but these terms don't paint much of a personality picture. How do you get to know God like you know your best friend whom you can see and touch, who smells when he sweats, snorts soda through his nose when laughing and makes strange gurgling noises while taking a nap? As I said before, the very characteristics that make God who he is also make it frustrating and difficult to get to know him personally.

Many of us are left struggling to find the personal relationship with God that others talk about with such ease. Feeling squeezed by religious peer pressure, we pretend to have something we don't. Inwardly we feel isolated, as if we were the only ones who wrestle to find God and hear his voice. We feel frustrated and abandoned while everyone around us seems to experience God effortlessly. We fumble around in the deafening silence while God speaks to everyone else about their everyday lives. Outwardly we fake it to keep up with others—who are probably doing the same thing. We build pretend denominations, pretend churches, pretend youth groups and pretend relationships. Afraid to ask the difficult questions, we become alienated from God—angry with him for treating us unjustly or condemning ourselves for being unworthy.

I have felt times of God's presence and absence, fullness and emptiness, intimacy and dark void. One of the darkest times in my soul was during my theological studies at seminary. I was immersed in an environment where we spent every day reading, thinking, studying and learning about God. One afternoon I was sitting in a little cubicle in the library, buried under a pile of books, when the thought flashed into my mind out of nowhere,

---

Is God real?

I felt the cold, icy grip of panic seize me—I could not answer the question. My mind felt numb. Regardless of my knowledge or past experiences, at that moment I felt as if I had nothing to hold onto. I had no idea whether or not God was real. I staggered around in a state of shock for about three weeks. No amount of reflection or persuasion seemed to help. I experienced a complete and utter crisis of faith. In desperation I cried out to the heavens, but they seemed as responsive as stone. My prayers seemed to bounce off the ceiling. God didn't rip the heavens open and swoop down in a chariot of fire; no stone tablets fell from the sky; there were no burning bushes or angelic visitations. The only answer was silence.

In time my old feelings returned, and I knew that God was real; but my questions were left unanswered. If God is a good Father who longs to be with us, why do we experience those devastatingly difficult wilderness-like times? What is going on during those times that often leave us feeling abandoned and frustrated, unable to figure out why it's even happening? Have you ever prayed and prayed to God in agonizing despair, only to feel lost and alone? Where is God at those times, and why doesn't he answer? Why does he seemingly speak to everyone else but ignore you? Have you ever thought that perhaps there was something wrong with you? Have you been left wondering if God even cares?

Though it was not a North American or European city, it looked and felt just like one. The smells and sounds of life in the fast lane are much the same wherever you go. The desperate pursuit of materialism and "the good life" consumed everyone. The culture was driven by the latest fashion trends. Every Friday and Saturday night, young men and women paraded around like peacocks, desperate to show off their latest outfits to prove they were cool. School was a devastating jungle that callously rejected those who didn't have designer jeans or the latest edition basketball shoes. Shops, magazines and commercials relentlessly bombarded society with their gospel of fashion and style. Either you squeezed into the mold, or you were a loser.

It was the "beautiful" culture, filled with exquisite clothes, shiny technology, stunning cosmetics, trendy hairstyles and overpriced juice and coffee. The simplicity of life had been obliterated by the drive to consume more and more stuff. Materialism was king. Few lives were gently led by the mystery of faith.

---

society was hollow. people were shells, unfulfilled and without hope.

In our day there's nothing too unusual about such a place. But this place wasn't in our day. It had been hundreds of years since creation. The world was dominated by beautiful people in pursuit of the beautiful life, and every inclination of these people was evil. Society was rampant with corruption and overflowing with violence. The human race had spiraled into such depravity and self-destruction that no redeeming features could be found.

The Father looked upon a wicked society that was so wrapped up in itself that it had forgotten its reason for existence. People had abandoned their loving creator. Faith and worship were hokey, merely superstitions held by unenlightened ancestors. The Father was so disappointed with the human race that he was sorry he had created it. His heart was filled with the stabbing pain of rejection and regret. He searched to and fro, desperate to find a remnant of goodness and faith. In all of creation only one man found favor in the Father's eyes.

His name was Noah.

Noah grew up in a bustling metropolis that had risen like a phoenix from the dust of the wilderness. He was a direct descendant of Adam—Adam's great-great-great-great-great-great-great-grandson. Adam had died at the ripe old age of 930, about a hundred years before Noah had been born. Perhaps everyone up until Noah had sat on Adam's knee as he told them all about those first days of humanity. Noah's would have been the first generation in his family to hear the creation story secondhand. He might have imagined what it would have been like to talk firsthand to Adam like his father Lamech had. He must have wondered what sort of man Adam was—the first human ever!

Noah was now nearly five hundred years old, and he was daydreaming. He felt his mind snap back into the moment as he sat at his desk, staring out of the window at the blue skies beyond. He was supposed to be preparing a sermon, but for the last half hour, he had been lost in thought as his mind drifted to a perfect place, the Garden of Eden.

He tried to refocus his mind to his sermon. *Oh, what's the point? Hardly anyone even comes to the services. No one cares.* Noah could not understand how his society had drifted so far from God. Generations of people who had known Adam personally were still alive. What was everybody thinking? Week in and week out, Noah prepared his sermons, only to deliver them to an empty house except for the odd homeless guy who came in to sleep on the back bench. Noah's heart broke for his nation. He felt so small, so isolated, so hopeless. He wondered if he was even doing the right thing. It all seemed like such a hard, lonely struggle.

Noah had experienced a revolution of grace.

He knew he could not earn acceptance from God. He could only receive the Father's freely given favor with a heart of gratitude. He could not help sharing his revolution with others; it just came out of him naturally. Everyone liked Noah. He always had an encouraging word or accepting smile. When people came to him for advice, he never made them feel bad. Instead he encouraged them that the Father would never stop believing in or searching for them. He had an easygoing, lighthearted, down-to-earth way about him that made people feel as if he really cared. Everyone liked Noah, but no one listened to him.

It was late in the evening. Noah was feeling sorry for himself. He mumbled his frustration as he prayed. No one had come to the service that morning—not even the homeless guy. Most people preferred to sleep in, read the paper, go to brunch or watch the big game. Noah halfheartedly prayed, *Sometimes I wonder if anything will ever change.* He sat in the silence. He was about to get up and turn the news on, when three words came to him:

"Build an ark."

He had no idea what it meant and was about to discount it when he heard it again. It was so strange. He ran his fingers through his hair. Noah wondered if fatigue was playing tricks on his mind. The phrase haunted him through the entire night. Later in bed he tossed and turned, desperate for sleep but unable to find a comfortable position. Finally he drifted off.

The early morning sunlight streamed in through the shutters and danced on Noah's eyelids. They fluttered briefly and slowly opened. He felt like he had hardly slept. His mind was groggy. It took him a minute to remember what day it was. Suddenly the words came again, "Build an ark." Noah stared at the fingers of light poking through the shutters. "Lord, is that really you?" Noah had no idea what was going on, but he knew God was trying to communicate with him. He wasn't sure how he knew, he just did.

"OK, Lord. But what's an ark?"

"A ship . . . OK . . . ummm, what's a ship?"

"Water, right . . . How big?!"

At around five hundred years old, Noah changed careers. His family was dumbfounded the day he came home and announced he had quit his job. They thought he was joking. No one had taken this ark thing seriously. What did he know about building ships? How would he make money and provide for his family if he quit his job? What did he mean that God had spoken to him? Where was God exactly?

How could he just give up everything he had ever worked for and go off on this folly?

Noah spent many sleepless nights thinking about his family's words. Was he abandoning his responsibilities? Would his family lose face in the community? Every time he closed his eyes, he saw the disappointment that had been on his father's face. Of all people, he thought Lamech would have understood. Noah felt the cold dread of fear. What if he failed? What if he ran out of money? What if his family was right? But he had to try. He had to trust God.

To begin with, he had to find a suitable place to build. The dimensions God had given him for this ship were enormous, and besides, he needed somewhere to store supplies. The main problem was the damp ground from the heavy dews and underground springs that watered the earth each day. It wouldn't take long for the dampness to rot the wood. He would have to find someplace dry, where the water would run off the ground where the ship stood. There was only one place suitable—the hill that had overlooked the Garden of Eden just outside town. He had walked up there many times, where only a few straggly bushes grew. But building the ark on that hill would also mean that it would be clearly visible to all for miles around.

Noah would work on the ark six days a week, eight to ten hours a day, for a hundred years. After he had cleared the ground on top of the hill, his next problem was timber. There were no trees up there. They were all in the valley down below. He had to cut down each tree by hand, saw every branch off and then drag the massive trunk all the way up the hill. He had to study physics. He would need at least two engineering degrees. Once he had the wood up the hill, he had to figure out how to mill it and turn it from tree trunks into planks of timber. He tried desperately to wrap his head around the sheer size of the project. The ark was to be three stories high inside. Four hundred and fifty feet long, forty-five feet high, seventy-five feet wide.

Noah sat on a tree trunk, overwhelmed. Where should he start?

He had to design new tools, invent new engineering principles and methods. Wood had to be shaped and fixed together to withstand massive amounts of weight and pressure. It took years to figure out load transference and framing techniques. Then there would be the problem of designing and building elaborate pulley systems to lift wood into place high inside. Thousands of days were spent building scaffolding that would ultimately surround and encase the vessel during construction.

Noah worked day after day, week after week, month after month, year after year.

It wasn't long before word got around. People came, driven by curiosity, to see the latest developments. Soon people from neighboring towns began to swing by and check out the progress. As people gathered and looked on in amazement, they must have thought that Noah was completely mad! He had quit his job, abandoned his friends and family and become immersed in this all-consuming task of building the world's largest oceangoing vessel—on the top of a hill, nowhere near water! No one could understand the concept of rain. Why build this massive floating structure with no possible way to move it after completion? He was an idiot.

Noah was like the town weirdo, living on the outskirts in a brightly painted camper with hundreds of garden gnomes littering his front yard and driving an old hand-painted bus that was covered in bumper stickers with crazy statements. As time passed, more and more people came and stood in awe at the utter insanity of it all. Noah was a laughingstock. People openly heckled him as he worked. Songs were released, jokes made their rounds, late-night talk show hosts made mincemeat out of him. He was constantly in the papers. One paper had a cartoon strip about him that ran for years. Busloads of onlookers would pull up on the weekends as people came from far and wide to see his work with their own eyes.

When people gathered, Noah would put down his hammer, stand on the scaffold and share why he was building this vessel of refuge and grace. He told them about the Father's heart, that God was still relentlessly pursuing them even though they didn't want to be found. He offered them forgiveness and hope. They too could experience the revolution of grace. He so desperately wanted people to experience the Father as he had. All they had to do was get on board.

---

people listened for hours, but no one got on board.

Morning after morning Noah would trudge up the hill in the predawn light only to find his work from the previous day smashed by vandals. He heaved a heavy sigh as he picked up the broken pieces to start over again. He felt overwhelmed by the task as he scrubbed away the latest graffiti that a gang of local youths had left the night before. People misunderstood him, despised him and wanted to see him fail miserably. His toolshed was constantly broken into. His timber was stolen. Time after time Noah would show up and find that he had taken two steps back.

Noah stood alone.

He would trudge home every evening with a heavy heart, but there was no one to share it with. His family didn't really understand. They thought Noah was a little obsessive with this whole ark thing. Why did he have to quit his job and spend every waking hour on that hill? His friends were confused. They felt hurt. He didn't have much time for socializing, and even when he did, what could they talk about? They felt abandoned and rejected by Noah. He cared more for his ark than he did for them. Wasn't he happy enough sharing his little sermons every week? Why did he have to take it all so seriously? Why did he have to take it so far? Didn't he care about his friends and family? Didn't he realize that he had become the town freak, that he was an embarrassment?

Sweat poured down his brow as he worked. Wiping it away with his sleeve, he put a few nails between his lips, grabbed his hammer from his tool belt and held a board in place. He tapped the first nail into position. Just as he was rearing his hammer back to pound the nail, he stopped. He stared at the nail. *What on earth am I doing here?* A tear welled up in the corner of his eye, and his bottom lip began to quiver. He felt so lost. Every day for nearly a hundred years Noah had awakened to clear blue skies and a growing and nagging sense of doubt. What was he doing?

This is stupid, **he thought to himself.** ***I can't make a difference. Why am I even here? I gave up everything for this?***

It had been so long since he heard those faint words calling him to build an ark. He wondered again if they had even come from God. Day in and day out, Noah woke to sunshine—and to misunderstanding and persecution. And every day, in the face of contradiction and ridicule, he worked on. How many countless nights did Noah lie awake, begging to hear from God? He ached for a word of confirmation—anything. It had been five years since he heard God's call. Ten years. Twenty-five years. Fifty years. Ninety-nine years had passed since Noah heard the still, small voice of God.

Noah waded through the dark, evil nights of confusion and temptation. Where was God? Why didn't he defend Noah? Was he upset? Had Noah misunderstood his will and strayed into this unforgiving wilderness? All Noah could do was reach out for God's hand and hold on for dear life as he endured the dark night of the soul.

When I was about twenty-three, I started coming home from work at night feeling exhausted. I was so tired I would fall into bed early in the evening, but when I woke the next morning, it didn't feel like I had rested at all. As the weeks passed I found myself exhausted at work. I had no energy. I would slump home and fall into bed. When I woke the next morning after a fitful night's sleep, rather than feeling rested I felt like I had run a marathon. I also developed headaches and severe pains in my joints, and my mind was so tired I would forget what I was saying midsentence. I went to the doctors, but they found nothing. There were days when I was too sick to get out of bed. Eventually things got so bad that I couldn't go to work.

I remember going to church during that time and sitting in the corridor. At first people would come and ask how I felt. One person suggested I was in some kind of spiritual training. Someone told me to count my blessings, as there were other people far worse off. I was told that if only I had more faith I would be healed. One person thought I was sick because of sin in my life. I repented. I repented so much that I ended up repenting of stuff I hadn't even done. When nothing changed, people accused me of not wanting to get better. Finally they stopped asking. It was always the quick fix they expected, and when one didn't come they decided there had to be something wrong on my end. In all of that time, no one ever simply sat down next to me and said, "I'm sorry for you. If you need someone to talk to, give me a call." Hurt, I became cynical and a bit depressed.

It was almost two years before I started to feel a little better. Finally I recovered to about seventy percent. I have been at seventy percent for about thirteen years now. Some days are better than others. I have forgotten what it's like to feel good or to wake up feeling refreshed. In the process, I have experienced the dark night of the soul or what we sometimes call the spiritual wilderness.

However, in those times of difficulty and despair, I have learned not to confuse life's problems with God.

Challenges in life do not mean that God is unfair or uninterested. If I assume that I will always be in good health and never have any disappointments or struggles, I am setting myself up for a fall. Those things will come. But the Father's existence, love and his relationship with me are not determined by my physical conditions.

On the contrary, I have found that I have grown closer to God as I have fellowshiped with him in my difficulties. At first I was so busy struggling to get out of the fire, I didn't realize that we encounter the Father *in* the fire. When three Hebrew boys were thrown into a fire, the king looked in and said, "Hold on, there's a fourth in there, and he looks like God" (see Daniel 3:25). Moses encountered God in the wilderness, not in the palace. We seek mountaintop experiences, but fruit doesn't grow on mountaintops; it grows in the valley.

As I stopped struggling to get out of these times as fast as I could, I found a deep fellowship with a loving Father. I clung to God because he was all there was. I was driven to a rich, abiding relationship with him that I would have missed otherwise. I have developed what I can only call a mystical union with Jesus. I discovered the Father's grace in the midst of weakness. When we come out on the other side of such times, we have a new connection with God in the quiet place of our heart and it is unshakable.

Had I not gone through those wilderness experiences, I would never have slowed down enough to discover the gift of God's grace. In fact, I look at such times themselves as gifts from the Father. They are the times of real growth in my life, times of deep connection with God. I believe he gives those times to us as and when we are ready to handle them. They are evidence of God's favor and trust, not of his abandonment. If you are going through or have gone through a wilderness experience, be encouraged. The Father has entrusted that period to you because he believes in you and longs to meet you at a new level. It is potentially the time of greatest growth in your life and comes directly from the Father's heart.

On the other side of such experiences, we find our relationship with God is no longer dependent upon circumstances. In time fruit is evident as we are able to connect with and encourage others who are going through the same thing. We are able to relate to them in genuine ways without discounting or glossing over their struggles. We are able to enter into their struggles and share a deep peace that has been forged in solitude. Just as with Noah, the real battle is not with the circumstances but within us.

The real battle is whether we will trust the Father.

The moment our faith feels the weakest, it is most active. In those moments our response—our choice—matters. It matters because we are involved in the battle of the cosmos as we struggle to see the kingdom of light push back the kingdom of darkness. The apostle Paul tells us that all creation is involved in this struggle. It groans as it waits for the sons and daughters of God, who will liberate and bring glorious freedom, to be revealed (Romans 8:18-25). Your struggle and my struggle matter. In moments when we feel lost and abandoned, we are right in the middle of the battle. Noah's choice made a difference. Our choices make a difference.

Rather than looking within and asking why this is happening, we need to look around and ask "What do I need to do now?"

Our participation in this struggle helps defeat the tyranny of pain and difficulty that we are struggling with.

But this isn't just a story about Noah; it is a story about me as I wonder if God has abandoned me in my struggle. And it isn't just a story about me; it's a story about the Father's heart. The Father has not abandoned us. He is not uninterested or uncaring. He is entrusting us with a gift: to see his kingdom come and to find a level of intimacy with him that we would otherwise never know. He offers us the path to maturity.

A father took his two sons tubing on the river for the first time. Holding hands, they linked together as they rode the white water, shouting and laughing. The next set of rapids was much stronger, and as they hit the whitecaps, they were tossed and pulled about. The power of the water tipped and pulled them from their tubes, flinging them like rag dolls.

The rapids pulled one of the boys down into the swell and then spat him onto the riverbank. He hit the bank with a thud and knocked his head on one of the rocks. As he regained consciousness, his head was spinning and he was dazed. Sounds were muffled and confusing as the water rushed past. Slowly he looked around the riverbank for his little brother and dad. They were nowhere to be seen. He looked farther up the bank and could see people running toward him, pointing and shouting.

They were pointing out into the river. His little brother was standing ankle deep in the middle of the river. The rapids were surging around his ankles as he stood crying. The older boy passed out again. He woke several hours later in the hospital. He panicked.

Sitting up in bed he tugged at the curtain beside him. He pulled it back to find his little brother lying in the next bed, gently weeping.

"Where's Daddy?" the older boy asked. "I was standing on his shoulders," replied his younger brother.

Later when the rescue crew dredged the river, they found that the father had wedged his feet between two rocks on purpose so his son could stand on his shoulders.

When the river is raging around us and we feel lost and abandoned, we are not alone—we are standing on our Father's shoulders. We might find it inexplainable, but he won't move. He has a single relentless stance toward us—he passionately loves us. It is a divine obsession.

OBSESSIVE BEHAVIOR

1. Which characteristics of God make it hardest for you to connect with him or trust him? In what ways do you struggle to find a personal relationship with God? How can that change?

2. List some of the ways you pretend around others. Why not discuss with friends or your small group how you can change that?

3. What was your last wilderness experience? Did you run to God or from him? Does knowing how much those times matter shed new light on them? How?

4. Do you feel that you have connected with God at a deeper level because of that experience, regardless of unanswered questions?

5. What do you think about God when he is silent? Do you ever think he might be listening to you?

6. Have you been able to use your experience to encourage others? How did that make you feel?

Jot down a few things you don't want to forget from this chapter.

1.

2.

3.

RELENTLESS PURSUIT

Father, I want my life for you to be as fanatical as yours is for mine, so I commit to . . .

Spend a few minutes talking to God about how you feel. List some specific prayer needs and action points that will help you live out the truths in this chapter.

where to from here?

NOW comes the hard part—moving all this from *head to heart.* You see, it's one thing to know this stuff in our heads, but it's another thing to let it take root deep down in our hearts and bring real transformation. But if we can reach out and touch God's heart, *it will change us.* I'm not a spiritual giant; in fact, I struggle with insecurity and lack of confidence. But the more I dare to believe that God is divinely obsessed with me—and not just with the person next to me—the more I sense myself touching the Father's heart, which transforms my own. Why not join me? Take that risky step of faith and dare to believe that this is how the Father feels about you, and allow his heart to overwhelm and transform yours.

One way to continue this journey of knowing the Father's heart is to consider dedicating six months to God at Youth with a Mission on a Discipleship Training School (DTS). A DTS is a life-changing experience to help you "know God and to make him known." It's a time for you to seek the Father-heart of God. Putting aside all the distractions of life, you can focus on Jesus and hear his heartbeat for the nations. It's a time to step out of your comfort zone and give God your whole heart—your whole life! It's a time to know God's heart for a hurting world and see him use *you* to reach those who are bruised and dying. I guarantee, after it you will never want to go back to the way you were.

If you would like more information about a DTS or about joining us for a short-term mission outreach, then contact us through our Web site, www.ywamwaves.com, or write to me personally at hensser@hotmail.com.